Ysenda Maxtone Graham is an author and journalist who has written widely for the *Spectator, Sunday Telegraph, Sunday Express* and *Evening Standard*, among many other publications. She is the author of *The Church Hesitant: A Portrait of the Church of England Today, The Real Mrs Miniver*, a biography of her grandmother Jan Struther, which was shortlisted for the Whitbread Biography of the Year in 2002, and *Mr Tibbit's Catholic School*, which has achieved the status of a minor classic since it was first published in 2011. She lives in London with her husband and their three sons.

'A rich read . . . Ysenda Maxtone Graham has drawn aside the curtain on the hermetic, arcane world of the mid-twentieth-century girls' boarding school, which we all believed to be weird, but few of us – unless we were there – realized was as eccentric, hilariously funny, cruel, terrifying, snobbish, rapturous and emotionally intense as the profoundly outlandish environment portrayed in these pages . . . *Terms & Conditions* is a funny, vivid and excruciating book, which has left me filled with admiration for the brave, damaged survivors of this lost world' Virginia Nicholson, *The Times*

'It's SO GOOD and hilarious and interesting. Am giving to all my old school friends for Christmas' India Knight

'A scintillating history of the mid-twentieth century girls' boarding school . . . this is by far the most entertaining book I have read this year' D. J. Taylor, *Oldie*

'If you think the St Trinian's films were fictitious, then this wonderful book will surely convince you that they were documentaries' Craig Brown, *Mail on Sunday*

'This vivid study of life at girls' boarding schools between 1939 and 1979 is both hilarious and poignant' *Country Life*

'The girls' boarding school! What a ripe theme for the most observant verbal artist in our midst today – the absurdly underrated and undersung Ysenda Maxtone Graham, who has the beadiness and nosiness of the best investigative reporter, the wit of Jane Austen and a take on life which is like no one else's. This book has been my constant companion ever since it appeared a few months ago' A. N. Wilson, *Evening Standard*

TERMS & CONDITIONS

Life in Girls' Boarding Schools,
1939–1979

YSENDA MAXTONE GRAHAM

ABACUS

First published in Great Britain in 2016 by Slightly Foxed Ltd.
This paperback edition published in 2017 by Abacus

1 3 5 7 9 10 8 6 4 2

A CIP catalogue record for this book
is available from the British Library.

ISBN 978-0-349-14306-4

Typeset in Garamond by M Rules
Printed and bound in Great Britain by
Clays Ltd, St Ives plc

Papers used by Abacus are from well-managed forests
and other responsible sources.

Abacus
An imprint of
Little, Brown Book Group
Carmelite House
50 Victoria Embankment
London EC4Y 0DZ

An Hachette UK Company
www.hachette.co.uk

www.littlebrown.co.uk

For my sister Livia

Contents

Preface

I went to a girls' boarding-school in 1972. It was only for an afternoon. I'd been staying with a friend for half-term and we stopped on our way into London to drop her older sister back at school. I can't remember which it was. Wycombe Abbey? Cobham Hall? Or Benenden, then of matchless fame for the education of Princess Anne? Though I'd never actually been inside a boarding-school, I knew all about them from books like *Third Form at Malory Towers* by the evidence-based historian, as I supposed she was, Enid Blyton. Boarding-schools were palaces of fun, emporia of midnight feasts and loyal mischievous friends. In the summer there would be lessons on the grass. In winter there would be snowballs and skating on the lake, heedless of the cries of Mam'zelle, the scatty French teacher whom everyone teased, anxiously bleating for us to be'ave! Girls! *S'il vous plait!* If the money could be found, I would join these happy folk before the year was out.

That day we drove up, not to the handsome manor-house that fronted the establishment, but round to an ugly annexe where a side door, fenestrated with chicken-wire glass, formed the pupils' entrance. Shushed by the suddenly meek and obedient-looking sister, we threaded in silence down mazes of low-ceilinged linoleum corridors. I remember the dingy lighting, the rows of closed doors with something unnervingly quiet behind them, the punitive ugliness of everything, and the billows of cooking cabbage-smell that rolled up the passageways and under the doors like smoke through a burning building.

I went to a London day school; and had forgotten this incident altogether until the glorious book you have in your hand, with its startlingly bright evocations of women's boarding-schools in the twentieth century, flushed it from the overgrowth of my memory. What an inspired idea of hers – to write a book on this under-exposed subject. Existing accounts are abundant but misleading. Indeed, as we learn in these pages, the shattering disappointment of little girls who had begged to be sent to boarding-school and were then faced with the reality was one of the most recurrent of all school memories and a common scar.

This is not a history of girls' boarding-schools. It's not easy to say where, exactly, you would shelve it. It could be under memoir. Or is it more like anthropology? Here's a study of a vanished society, based upon the testimony of elders whose way of life has been erased by exposure to modern culture, but who remember the days before the first boats came upriver. The other option would be comedy, as it's the funniest book you'll read all year, and if it doesn't win the P. G. Wodehouse prize, there is no justice in the world.

YMG's 'elders' in this case are a cohort of women who already know there is no justice in the world, as they went to school in 'the last years of the boarding-school olden days'. They attended establishments all along the academic scale, from the arid Cheltenham Ladies' College to the jolly place where a 'lab.' meant a labrador. They are witnesses to a lost era, when hot-water bottles were made of ice, pudding of 'phlegm', and girls' education was, in the main, so far subsumed to that of their brothers that fear of 'putting husbands off' with too much of it was an important consideration for the makers of their timetables. The oldest of them were schooled in the 1930s. As for the youngest, YMG decided,

My cut-off date ... would be the advent of the duvet. As soon as duvets, with their downy warmth and tog-factors, came into fashion, I would be out. This was in about 1979, the introduction of duvets coinciding with the Thatcher era. The girls' boarding-school in the age of the duvet is another matter entirely from the girls' boarding-school in the age of the frozen hot-water bottle.

A lost world, and also a closed one. It is now unimaginable that parents would consign their offspring for months and even years, if the parents lived far away, with no questions asked and no contact but the occasional censored letter, to a place they had chosen from a photograph in a prospectus, or because 'the quality of the toasted tea cake' at the open day had made an impression upon them. But so it was: much of what is described here could only occur in an environment almost completely shut off from outside interference and therefore free to breed self-perpetuating systems, preoccupations, rules and taboos so arcane and downright bonkers that if an ex-girl is rash enough to mention them in adult life, no one will believe her. YMG suggests this is something to do with women:

> Anyone who has ever compared a convent with a monastery will have noticed that women tend to make more rules than men. Compare the way the genial monks at the Community of the Resurrection at Mirfield wolf down their supper and chat (they pronounce 'pizza' as 'pitzer') while the West Mailing nuns nibble their bread and marge in silence.

Few authors would have such a fruitful comparison at their command; but one comes to expect it from YMG. As I turned the pages and bits of boarding-school life were unearthed piecemeal, like the skeleton of some fantastic and once-common beast, I began to imagine what an index would look like:

Bosoms, books and bath cubes. Who now remembers
bath cubes, that most Spartan of bath-time luxuries, the
main point of which was to disguise the rusty patches of
bath enamel under your bottom with their own indissoluble
sandiness? Let alone that they once had currency as single
enticements.

YMG has been fortunate in her examples of Boarding-
School Woman: a type of adult female who, her researches
reveal,

sleeps with the window wide open; feels homesick on
Sunday evenings even though she is now at home; never
touches cauliflower cheese; keeps an old address book
in which most of the addresses have been there for so
long that they don't have postcodes; knows the Matins
Collects by heart; fears unpopularity even among fully
grown women in middle age; and still associates Friday
with the smell of fish.

If this sample is representative, then Boarding-School Woman is also funny and thoughtful – and clever, in spite of the exertions of her school. Also, possessed of perfect memory. The women here have near-eidetic recall of their schooldays and we must all be grateful that YMG has got to them in time to pluck their collective experience from the waters of oblivion. They don't remember things in the way a non-boarder might expect. Who'd suppose that one of the very worst horrors a boarding-school could inflict was, by general agreement, 'the mistress who wanted to be your friend'? And that grown women would still be shuddering forty years later at the memory of this menace: 'you thought she might take your hand and stroke it'?

Physical and emotional privations, on the other hand, are shrugged off, as are the many ingenious acts of sadism in these pages. YMG detects a remarkable lack of self-pity in her sample of Old Girls: they do not see themselves as 'victims' or 'survivors' of any kind and would hate to be regarded as such. The only time anyone really seems angry is when the question of what had happened when they left school came up. Some women from the 'book-learning puts husbands off' type of establishment felt that the neglect of their education, be it wilful or careless, had hobbled them for life.

It wasn't necessarily the fault of the schools. Schools are among the slowest of entities to register social change. Ideas and textbooks are only replaced when absolutely necessary and the traditional practice is to prepare the current generation of pupils for the lives of the preceding one. When change is rapid and unprecedented, as happened with women's expectations in the twentieth century, this matters more.

I doubt a better chronicler of these times could be found than YMG. As an alumna of Sibton Park Preparatory School for Girls, she has had experiences with cauliflower that have left her with a fine sense of sympathetic discrimination. She is not one for over-emoting, and nothing seems to leave her aghast. The incidents of cruelty appear without comment – they stand on their own merits – and we often sense a muffled cheer for school eccentricities and the kind of resilient woman they produced.

There's a different sort of sensitivity at work in YMG: a genius for comedy, and also a kind of comic pathos that leaves us not knowing whether to laugh or cry. For example, when she points out the deployment of capital letters in school literature, or School Literature, as a form of reverence for school creeds ('three grey School Cardigans' on a terrifying clothes list). Or when she exhumes a gem like Miss Alice Baird's letter to her sixth form at St James's, West Malvern, in the 1930s: 'I sometimes speak about the *dry rot* of slackness ... ' begins Miss Baird, and instantly we are there in West Malvern with her. We can well imagine the rolling eyes of the poor sixth-former reading this; but we can also picture Miss Baird writing it from the confines of her prospects between the wars: the changeless timetable of the years, the aeons of tenure implied in that 'I sometimes speak'; the note of self-estimation she permits herself in resorting to her own *mot juste*.

St James's has since merged with three other schools in the vicinity of West Malvern and is one of the girls' boarding-schools 'still going strong' today, as YMG puts it, with the faintly subversive qualifier, 'though some of them can only keep going by bringing in a large number of girls from overseas'. If you look it up you'll find it now offers show-jumping, drama and a fashion show to girls who can choose 'to stay with us all week, all term, or drop in for a night now and then'. Drop in. *Drop in*, under the very portrait of Miss Baird. I do hope these girls all get *Terms & Conditions* for Christmas, to show them how lucky they are. In fact, I hope everyone gets *Terms & Conditions* for Christmas, as it will make a joy of Boxing Day.

NICOLA SHULMAN

Introduction

Girls, Old Girls and Very Old Girls

She sleeps with the window wide open all year round; feels homesick on Sunday evenings even though she is now at home; never touches cauliflower cheese; keeps an old address book in which most of the addresses have been there for so long that they don't have postcodes; knows the Matins Collects by heart; fears unpopularity even among fully-grown women in middle age; and still associates Friday with the smell of fish. She has a soft spot for carpeted rooms; is an accomplished maker of beds and thinks fitted sheets are cheating; knows how to cast on and off in knitting; and still thinks there is something exciting about a parcel arriving by post, even if it's just a consignment of Hoover bags from Amazon. She's proud that once (but only once) she made a whole long-sleeved silk blouse; she uses the adjective 'super' decades after it has gone out of fashion; can do 'the devil's fork' in cat's cradle; when in France says 'Mamzelle' rather than 'Mamm-euh-zelle'; still slightly dreads a hairwash; and feels nauseous when accosted by the smell of wood polish on a stairwell.

She belongs to the genus 'Woman Who Went to a British Girls' Boarding-School', and in this book I shall try to capture her kind and the establishments she attended. Since starting to study the subject of girls' boarding-schools and the women who went to them within living memory – a small but distinct fraction of the British population, and one not often in the limelight – I think I've become adept at spotting such a person in the crowd: at least, if she is above the age of 55. She has a certain inner toughness about her, which peeps out from her ageing face. I can tell, from her posture and her calves, whether she was good or bad at games. She might be riding a bicycle with a basket up a London street, or requesting a new biography or Christmas cookbook at the local independent bookshop (the height of the book's brow depending on the blueness of her stocking), or producing her recyclable bags at the supermarket till, or looking for a blind (plain or chintzy) in the soft furnishings department at John Lewis, and I wonder: Which one did you go to? Did you walk in a crocodile to church on Sunday mornings? Did your dormitory win the Tidiness Cup? Did you love or hate the endless afternoons on the lacrosse pitch? And do you pronounce it 'lacrosse' or 'la-crawsse'?

The character traits I mention above are not those of every

boarding-school girl. For example, five years of enforced finishing up of one's Saturday-evening cauliflower cheese can send a person in two directions. Either she finds she can eat anything put in front of her for the rest of her life, never makes a fuss and gets annoyed with other people who do; or she can go to the other extreme and live an adulthood of extreme pickiness. I know of one ex-boarding-school girl who won't allow a cauliflower into her house. Likewise, years of enforced sleeping with the window wide open in winter, so that a gale blew through the dormitory and you had to crack the ice in the basin in the morning, can turn a person either into someone who can't now get to sleep unless the window is wide open, or someone who has to have the central heating in the bedroom turned up high even in June, and an electric blanket too. Cicely Taylor, vivacious and bicycle-riding ex-Wycombe Abbey girl, who takes middle-aged people on cultural tours on ships (and who took me on a tour round the vast grounds of Wycombe Abbey), told me that some of the ex-boarding-school members of her travelling party get 'very uptight' when they discover they can't open the window of their cabin. They really would prefer to be soaked with sea-spray than deprived of fresh air.

The overriding trait seems to be a deep love of home, and a keen sense of the difference between home and school, or between home and any other institution. It occurred to me when researching this book that the word 'homely' needed to be invented only because children were sent *away* from home. It was used as a weapon of persuasion, both by

prospectuses trying to woo new girls, and by parents breaking the news to their daughters that they were going to be
sent to a 'lovely homely school in a big country house'. In
my researches I would come to see just how wide a spectrum
the word 'homely' could cover.

Women who have been to boarding-schools live with
flashbacks both joyous and nightmarish: more vivid than
daygirls' flashbacks because there was no daily escape. These
women – and I'm included, because I went to Sibton Park
Preparatory School for Girls in Lyminge, near Folkestone in
Kent, from 1972 to 1975 and have the brown velvet beret and
gingham overall to prove it – are still kept awake at night
by a recurring procession of ancient but still raw injustices
to do with hymn-books, vests and sudden confiscations.
Arriving at the houses of my interviewees, all ready to fire
away with a question about how many Bunsen burners the
school had in 1952, I was often assailed by a sharp memory
to do with knickers: knickers that had to be worn over
knicker linings; the difference between summer knickers
and winter knickers; the humiliation of one's knicker elastic
'going'; the desire to conform and wear the official school
knickers rather than the slightly different type one's mother
chose because she didn't hold with going to the official
uniform shop; the time someone had to write a letter of
apology to the school laundry because she said she had sent
her knickers to the wash but in fact that had been a white
lie; knickers that only went to the wash once a week, and
bloomers that only went once a fortnight. These are the

memories that really stay with a person. And these were just the kinds of details I was hoping to catch in my year of travelling round the country interviewing Old Girls in order to create a patchwork of twentieth-century boarding-school life in words.

The first Old Girl I interviewed, Jane Longrigg (b. 1929), lived in a cottage near Junction 5 of the M3. 'Turn right at the duck pond,' she said on the telephone, and I thought, 'This is how it starts and this is how it will go on: I will turn right at a great many duck ponds.' Eventually I bought a satnav which knew the duck ponds were coming.

'I ran away from Mrs Fyfe's when I was 14,' Jane Longrigg said, putting her sticks aside as we sat at her kitchen table piled high (as many Old Girls' kitchen tables are) with dog-eared reading matter.

'You ran away? Was this in about 1942?'

'Yes. Bubble Carew-Pole said to me, "Do let's run away. I've got a hired Daimler coming. With a chauffeur." The Daimler arrived, we were whisked off, and we went to see a film in Royston. We came out in the dark and there was nothing much to do in Royston so we decided to go back to school. No one had noticed we were missing.'

It sounded like the beginning of *The Lion, the Witch and the Wardrobe*, when no one noticed that Lucy had been to Narnia for the afternoon. But in this case, time in our world really had passed, and no one at Mrs Fyfe's had noticed the absence of the two girls. It gave me a glimpse of a long, lazy 1940s afternoon in a world far from the Blitz, where girls of high birth rambled free in vast country houses and their extensive grounds, not being taught very much and vaguely expected to grow up into young ladies with perfect manners who would marry dukes. The official name of Mrs Fyfe's was Longstowe Hall. It was in Cambridgeshire but later the school moved to Gloucestershire where it became Hatherop Castle.

'Was there a Mr Fyfe?'

'Yes, there was,' said Jane Longrigg, 'but not in my time. He'd gone out on to the lake one day to test the water to see if it was suitable for the girls to skate on. He fell through the ice and was never seen again. All that were found were his hat and his stick.'

So no one was keeping an eye on him, either. I would hear more about Mrs Fyfe from girls who were at Hatherop Castle under her reign in the 1960s, by which time she was very deaf and the girls would shout into her hearing-aid which looked like a cassette player and she would say, 'Please, no smut, my darlings.' Always, the tragic story of the disappearing Mr Fyfe hung there in the background.

As I drove away from Jane's cottage, I knew my investigation into Life in British Girls' Boarding-Schools was launched: but how could I do justice to the subject? So many schools, so many Old Girls. Think how many must have been to Wycombe Abbey alone, if it started in 1896 and is still going strong and has houses called Pitt, Rubens,

Airlie, Barry, Butler, Campbell, Cloister, Shelburne and Wendover. A whole book could be written just about that one school – and indeed it has, and I've read it. It's called *Wycombe Abbey: A Partial History* and it was written by the school's legendary spinster English teacher and Shakespeare-worshipper Lorna Flint, or 'Miss Flint', of whom we shall hear more. It is because of her that a whole generation of Wycombe-educated women never, ever use the word 'nice' or write 'Bucks' on an envelope – always 'Buckinghamshire'. I think Miss Flint must have been pleased when she came up with the book's title, with its *nice* double-meaning of 'partial'. I decided to have a start date and a cut-off date for the book's main span. The start date would be 'in living memory'. This is not a book about – for example – how Cheltenham Ladies' College was founded in 1853 and run by the great Dorothea Beale; that, too, has been written and it's called *A History of the Cheltenham Ladies College*, by A. K. Clarke. We'll hear in passing how many of the schools did start; but I don't want to bore the reader with too much 'It was agreed that a memorandum should be prepared on the constitution and duties of the increasingly influential Finance and General Purposes sub-committee.'

Nearly every famous girls' school has its own written history, and I've been collecting 'boring sentences from girls' school histories' while researching this book, and have been delighting in them in their own way. In their very boringness – their meticulous recording of too much information – they express the devotion felt by the author (nearly always an Old Girl or ex-mistress at the school) for every aspect of the beloved institution. Nothing is too small to record. Each time a new stained-glass window is donated to the dining-hall by a grateful Old Girl (and it's often), the event is recorded. So is every change-round of rooms, for example this one at the Scottish school St Leonards:

> It was now possible to increase the accommodation in the school by turning the old School Room into the Sixth Form Room and, by means of a staircase linking the first floor of the House with the school building, the large room, formerly a dormitory, on that floor became the staff-room.

It didn't occur to the writer that her readers might skim over that bit. Monica Beardsworth, Old Girl of Penrhos College for girls in Wales, and author of a slim volume called *Penrhos: The Second Fifty Years*, wins the prize for 'passage in a girls' school history with the most capital letters for non-proper nouns'. It describes a garden party in 1930 in which, 'perhaps inevitably, the weather took a hand'. (Historians of girls' schools would never say anything as blunt or unladylike as 'it rained'.)

> The marquee dripped; the bunting hung bedraggled, and the little tables were rushed into the Dining Hall. Massed Drill and Dancing Displays followed this Garden Party, and in the evening a short, informal Concert was given

by Old Penrhosians. With the majority of the School on their way to bed, the Staff and some of the Senior Girls replaced the chairs and put the Hall to rights so that it was ready for the Sunday Morning Service the next day. The Service, which was crowded ('Crush' Sunday, the school's nickname for these occasions, was singularly apposite), was conducted by the Rev. H. Lefroy Yorke, and at the Evening Service, a father of one of the girls, the Rev. T. Batty, vicar of All Saints, Coventry, officiated.

It's like reading a paragraph in German, in which all nouns do have capitals. Capital letters are used in girls' school histories as an expression of reverence. Lorna Flint herself wins the prize for 'author so steeped in school jargon it doesn't occur to her that a sentence seems decidedly odd':

The headmistress enjoyed reading or talking to Early or Late Beds.

Although I'll be making reference through such books to the earliest days of some of the schools, my real starting date is about 1939 – though one or two of the Very Old Girls I interviewed were sent to board just before the war.

My cut-off date, I decided, would be the advent of the duvet. As soon as duvets, with their downy warmth and tog-factors, came into fashion, I would be out. This was in about 1979, the introduction of duvets coinciding with the Thatcher era. The girls' boarding-school in the age of the duvet is another matter entirely from the girls' boarding-school in the age of the frozen hot-water bottle. It was not the centrally heated, duvet age I was interested in but the ice-age. The years I longed to capture were the last years of the boarding-school Olden Days – the last gasp of the Victorian era, when the comfort and happiness of children were not at the top of the agenda.

I yearned for stories about the coldness of schools. Another Longstowe Hall Old Girl, Mary-Ann Denham (aged 88), held up the crooked and still-red index finger of her right hand to me: it had never recovered from the chilblains she contracted there. 'There was no heating at all until four in the afternoon when they lit a stove,' she said. 'We did all our lessons wrapped up in rugs, with mittens on. But I had to have *this* hand out, in order to write.' Old Girls told me how they used to put their small allocated piece of floor-carpet on to their beds to add another layer to the pitiful sheets and blankets, as well as their heavy woollen school cloaks, to which they were addicted. Evacuated to Chatsworth in the war, Nancie Park picked her hot-water bottle off the floor in the morning and found it was a solid lump of ice.

Another reason for the 1979 cut-off date is that I wanted to make clear that this book is not a brochure – or any kind of anti-brochure – for the boarding-schools mentioned, many of which are still thriving, and deserve to be. Any 1970s trouble I might mention, when discipline and achievement started to fall apart, has now either been rectified or the school in question has closed.

You can spend happy hours browsing the websites of today's dazzling girls' boarding-schools; I urge you to do this once you've read this book, and you'll see just how different it all is nowadays. The schools look mouthwatering, with their purpose-built theatres, heated pools and girls playing the saxophone and making eco-cars. You can read the headmistress's introductory letter, or click on to a video of her speaking about how she never ceases to be amazed by what the girls manage to achieve in the school's nurturing environment, one that seeks to empower and bring out the very best in 'each and every girl'. You click on to the different boarding-houses and each one has a 'vibrant, happy atmosphere' and is 'a home from home for all our 66 girls'. Then you click on to the section called 'academic', and there's a photograph of girls in safety-goggles in the lab and a list of how many A*s they achieved in physics, chemistry and biology A-levels last year. We're now in the days when boarding-school girls aim to become doctors rather than nurses.

Yes: the great girls' boarding-schools are still going strong, although some of them can only keep going by bringing in a large number of students from overseas. Some have had to merge to survive. For example, Malvern Girls' College is now called Malvern St James, or 'MSJ'. The school is a merger not only of Malvern Girls' College and St James's, West Malvern, but also of the Abbey School and Lawnside.

It's slightly heartbreaking to read the blurb in the 'A bit of history' section of the websites of these merged schools: it demonstrates how, in any merger, there's always a dominating force that swallows up the weaker. 'The name of Lawnside is celebrated in one of the two main meeting rooms in Malvern St James,' we're told. Can it really be that the whole great school of Lawnside, with its traditions and its legendary pearly headmistresses, has been reduced to the mere name of a meeting room? One of Lawnside's proudest memories was that Elgar himself once jumped over the birdbath. But one Old Girl I interviewed would be pleased about its demotion: she loathed Lawnside, and is still traumatized by memories of her vicious English teacher who wrote 'Cliché, cliché, cliché, cliché, cliché' down the margin of her essay.

I didn't want the marketing departments of these schools to think I was writing about how the schools are now, or to mention my 'plug' on their newsflash for the day, or in any kind of press release, or on the continuous slide show on the television screen above the school's reception desk. I'm writing about the mid-twentieth-century past, in which there were no marketing departments and no screens, apart from the roll-down screen for the film on Sunday night, with projector and reel: a reel which, as Lizie de la Morinière (Hatherop Castle, early 1960s) remembers, 'broke six times during *A Night to Remember*, and which old Mr Wetherby, the school chauffeur, who was so fat he could hardly get in and out of the car, had to stick back together with Sellotape'.

*

Like many Old Girls, my fascination with girls' boarding-schools began with reading Angela Brazil's novels, in which gymslip-wearing girls, instead of saying 'Let's go!' said 'Scooterons-nous'. I will also admit to a childhood fascination with books about cruel English orphanages: an early form of *Schadenfreude*, because the worse the food was (thin, lumpy porridge in Noel Streatfeild's *Thursday's Child* or, in the case of poor punished Bonnie in Joan Aiken's *The Wolves of Willoughby Chase*, 'nothing to eat all day but two raw onions'), the more I liked reading about it. The craze for this misery-literature started when I was at a girls' boarding-school myself, so I think it was more a form of one-upmanship: I liked reading about girls who were having an even worse time than I was. I cried at 12.55 on my third Friday when I knew the fish-pie ordeal was about to begin; but it could have been worse. At least I had parents.

Reading the happier kind of school stories such as Brazil's novels, Enid Blyton's Malory Towers and Elinor Brent-Dyer's Chalet School books was another matter entirely. This was aspirational literature in which girls' boarding-schools were portrayed as wondrous places brimming with adventure, where you would make character-forming friendships and live for the honour of the school. Many of my interviewees devoured these books as children, and some of them begged their parents to be allowed to go to boarding-school because they wanted to go to just such a paradise, ideally in a manor house in Cornwall, with a locked-up room in the attic in which they would discover the treasure which actually belonged to one of the girls who had been cheated out of her inheritance ... and there would be picnics on the cliffs, lessons out of doors in the summer term, sketching classes with the art mistress, and with any luck 'a blackberry foray' in which the girls would saunter out into the countryside with their baskets and someone would get into a scrape. When my interviewees arrived at the actual schools, they had a great deal of time to measure their hopes against the reality in which they found themselves.

How did these *non*-fictional girls' schools begin? Whereas Winchester College was founded by a medieval bishop, for a king, and Eton shortly afterwards by an actual medieval monarch, girls' boarding-schools tended to be started, almost by accident, by two unmarried daughters of a wid- owed Victorian clergyman, who needed to 'take in' a few pupils in order to pay the bills. These sisters were often called Maud or Millicent, women with unflagging energy and small waists, who had a vision of how a girls' school should be, and who brought their schools into existence through dogged determination, enlisting wealthy professional men (often cousins) to form the necessary company and invest in the enterprise. These women were driven by zeal for the idea that girls could be properly educated together, as were their brothers. They thrived on obstacles in their way. The historians of their schools say things like, 'All this might have daunted lesser mortals than the Wingfield-Digbys.'

One particular girls'-school history caught my eye in the extensive history-of-schools section at the London Library, nearly all of which is taken up with weighty histories of boys' schools with titles like *Five Hundred Years a School*. It's called *I Was There*. As thick as the Bible, it tells the story of the founding and early years of the above-mentioned St James's, West Malvern. As well as describing exactly what girls learned to say in elocution lessons – 'An Irish squire in the West of Ireland was sitting by the fire with his violin when the choir-master entered with a bunch of violets' – it gives a glimpse of the romance and the rapture of girls' boarding-schools at the time of their small-scale beginnings.

Here we see the unmarried Baird twins, Miss Alice and Miss Katrine, both Newnham-educated, opening their new school for girls at Southbourne-on-Sea, Dorset in September 1896. On that momentous first day, when the doors opened, they had no pupils at all. It was a long, quiet wait, but by half-term they had secured one day-girl, Irene Bell. By January 1897 they had acquired two boarders. By the end of the first year they had eleven pupils, 'enough for a hockey team'. In the season 1899–1900 'a professional coach came to coach the First XI' – suggesting that there were now enough pupils to have a Second XI. Like many such schools, this one moved premises from a suburban house to a larger one in the country: in this case to St James's on a hillside outside Malvern, an impressive pile cleverly snapped up by the undauntable Bairds.

I Was There: the book's title captures the thrill of having been present at the school's dawn. Here are the recollections of a new girl describing the first term at the West Malvern premises: you can hear her rapturous voice and the fresh air in her lungs:

> I think we went a little wild on those first few days in this wonderful new school. I remember it as a time of rushing. Rushing down the wide steps into the green depths of the garden, rushing through the cloisters, down the Blue Drive, along the grass walks to the hockey field. As a result of too much rushing, a host of new rules speedily came into force.

Ah, yes: rules, and a host of them. That was to become a theme. Another pioneer, Penelope Lovell, focuses on the sounds of those early days:

> Summer sound of ball and racquet on the top tennis court. 'Yours!' 'Sorry!' 'Out!' 'Fifteen-all!' Somewhere Haines is mowing. 'Ker-slunk, ker-slunk, ker-slunk.' Two pianos are audible; one is having trouble with arpeggios, and from the distant swimming bath comes the heavy creak and thud of the diving board, the momentous splash; someone is practising for her Bronze medal.

It makes you wish you were there, right now – even if the water in the swimming bath was 53 degrees Fahrenheit, and acquiring a Bronze medal meant somersaulting over a daunting piece of Swedish gym apparatus. Miss Baird comes across as the ideal Angela Brazil-style headmistress, strict but kind and living entirely for the school and her girls. There's just one note that jars with the modern reader when Miss Baird, in one of the sections written by her in 1937, puts the word 'jobs' into inverted commas:

> I do not know at what stage Old Girls interest me most. For instance, whether it is when they have just left the chrysalis stage after a time in Paris or Munich or Florence, and they come down here to dazzle us with their transformation. Or whether it's when they come and tell us about varied and interesting courses of training or 'jobs' which they are doing so efficiently. Or, at another stage, when they come down as mothers of Present Girls.

We'll hear more about exactly what jobs, or 'jobs', Old Girls got up to when they left schools like these. We'll see to what extent a grandiose school motto such as Sherborne Girls' 'Great the hope and grand the prize' reflected reality.

Before we start, a quick word on surnames. I've decided not to use 'née', as I've come across it so much in school magazines for Old Girls giving news of what they're up to, and I find it rather diminishing. When these magazines mention (for example, and this one is made-up) 'Laura Finch (Hannington-Perry), Lovell, '53', you feel the poor woman is being brutally summed up: 'used to have double-barrelled surname, married Finch and lost it, was in Lovell (useless house) and is pushing 75'. It's even worse when there's *no* surname in brackets, which means that the woman never married. ('*Still* Plackett?' as Joyce Grenfell memorably said to a solitary fellow Old Girl outside the imagined tea-tent in her boarding-school-reunion sketch.) 'Née' is only of interest to the small number of contemporaries of the person mentioned. Old Girls' magazines need 'née' but this book doesn't. I'm using current surnames. Some of the people you will meet are famous and some are not: they are all equally important to the story.

Now, imagine you are a mother or father, on the veranda in the stifling heat of a Delhi afternoon in the late 1930s: you need to send your daughter to school in England next year. Which school will you choose?

1

Choosing a Suitable School

A gale of British fresh air would hit you in the face if you were such an expatriate wife and mother on your colonial veranda, leafing through the essential Truman & Knightley Schools Directory. Hundreds of schools placed advertisements in this thick annual hardback, and they vied with each other on three selling points: healthiness of position, well-drainedness of soil, and a willingness to take 'entire charge' of children whose parents lived abroad.

'The soil is sand and gravel and the climate is bracing...'

'Known for its invigorating air ...'

'Delightfully situated in the uplands of Hertfordshire ...'

'In the most beautiful part of Surrey, sometimes

called the "Switzerland" of England, it stands in its own grounds of 84 acres . . .'

'Special attention is given to backward and delicate girls, and the climate is well suited to children from India and other tropical countries, of whom entire charge is taken.'

'Yes,' these mothers decided, reading these mouthwatering descriptions, 'my daughter will be much better off at a place like that, mixing with other English girls. We mustn't let her go *native* here.' The directory's grainy black-and-white photographs of girls in bathing-caps lined up along the edge of freezing-looking outdoor pools positively attracted these too-hot parents.

The number of establishments to choose from was bewildering: in the late 1930s there were 16 private girls' schools in St Leonards, 22 in Malvern, 23 in Eastbourne, 32 in Bexhill-on-Sea and about 150 in Surrey. There were nine girls' boarding-schools called St Margaret's: in Bushey, Buxted, Folkestone, Hampstead, Harrow, Hindhead, Hythe, Hastings and Westgate-on-Sea. (In general, if the saint was female, so was the school: St Monica's, St Margaret's, St Anne's. Boys' schools were St Peter's and St Anthony's.) Some of these schools looked like stately homes; some looked like asylums; some looked like golf-clubhouses; but all of them thrived, with small numbers of girls, lots of maids, and fees of 36 guineas per term.

*

Going native was exactly what Ann Leslie seemed to her mother to be doing in Pakistan in the mid-1940s. Her father was stationed in Rawalpindi, as a soldier. Ann grew up speaking to the servants and their children in fluent Urdu in Pakistan, and in fluent Pashto in Afghanistan, where the family also lived for a while, and she never wore pants or shoes, 'because if you do in a hot climate you grow all kinds of bacteria'. Her favourite person in the world was her father's chief bearer, Yah Mahommed. 'I loved climbing on his back. He was a devout Muslim and used to pray five times a day. I did get into terrible trouble for climbing on to his back *while* he was praying.'

All this was not suitable, in the eyes of Ann's wildly beautiful mother. 'Theodora had many wonderful qualities,' Ann told me as we sat in a café near Haverstock Hill in Hampstead, 'but motherhood wasn't one of them. I once overheard her saying, "I cannot believe I gave birth to such a *plain* child."' At the age of 4 Ann was sent to board at St Hilda's Church of England school in 'Ooty', short for Ootacamund. 'It was a simulacrum of Wiltshire in the Nilgiri Hills of India, and had an area known as the Wenlock Downs. The houses were ersatz Victorian villas with names like Balmoral. I adored it, although sending a little girl away to school just after her fourth birthday would now be considered child abuse.'

But her parents, being Catholic, decided it was not right for their daughter to be at a Church of England school at which her best friend was actually a Muslim girl called Durr whose father had four wives, 'mostly not on speaking terms with each other'. So in late August 1952 Ann and her mother boarded a ship to Tilbury, where Ann shared a cabin with the Dagenham Girl Pipers, while her mother entertained the Captain.

After chugging into Tilbury docks, mother and daughter took a slow train to Matlock in Derbyshire. Why Matlock? Ann's mother had done minimal research into schools. She had chosen the Presentation Convent in Matlock for reasons of religion and health: it looked (in the directory) like a bracing Catholic school, in a spa-town on the edge of the Peak District, ideal for a delicate girl: Ann did suffer from bouts of pneumonia. She kissed Ann goodbye at the door and didn't see her for a year. Ann got into instant trouble with some of the nuns for not wearing pants. They thought she was depraved.

Health and happiness do not necessarily go together. For reasons of gravel soil and bracing air, girls found themselves washed up at places like the Presentation Convent at Matlock for years on end. We'll hear more about life at the Presentation Convent (and other Catholic establishments) in the chapter called 'Teaching Nuns and Kitchen Nuns'. Luckily, there were three extremely good teaching nuns in Matlock; and because Ann's father had read Greats at Oxford and wanted his daughter to learn Latin, she went once a week to a 'wizened old chap in town' for Latin lessons.

These days, when mothers spend every waking hour, and some of the sleeping ones too, agonizing about the perfect fit of school for their beloved daughter, and talking about little else to their friends for years, it's hard to imagine the lack of research conducted by prospective parents of seventy years ago. The education of sons was taken more seriously: parents did at least take into account the academic standard of the school. With girls, it was often simply a matter of finding a place where she would make suitable friends, learn good manners and perhaps eventually marry one of the suitable friends' eligible brothers.

There was a general unspoken feeling among upper-class parents that children were in just as much danger of 'going native' at home in rural England as they were in Rawalpindi. Going native meant spending all afternoon in the garden in a make-believe world. 'Kenneth, these children will be so *odd* if they don't go away to school,' Rosie de Courcy's mother said to her husband in 1962. Rosie and her sister had been educated by a governess till the age of 9, and they had a blissful life in their Gloucestershire country house and garden, mostly spent making puppets: 'hobby-horse after hobby-horse,' as Rosie said, 'inspired by *Hobby Horse Cottage* by Miss Read'. It was to save them from a life of perceived oddness that their parents decided to pluck Rosie and her sister out of that paradise and send them to Lawnside, where lots of their friends' children went and the girls would 'widen their acquaintance'. Widen their acquaintance? Well, up to a point. They would make friends with girls of their own class from all over the British Isles who travelled hundreds of miles to go to schools like Lawnside. But being plucked out of their home Garden of Eden meant goodbye to any chance of playing behind the greenhouses with the gardener's sons, and goodbye to any traces of a local accent you might pick up from such fraternizing. Your acquaintance would be widened and severely narrowed at the same time. 'And we've been wondering ever since,' said Rosie, 'why our parents decided to send us to such a *silly* school.'

'The great thing was,' as Gillian Charlton-Meyrick said to me when I asked her about postwar life at Oxenford (a happy, unambitious country school in Midlothian run by the sister of the Earl of Stair), 'we all came out of the same hatbox.'

I liked the idea of 'the same hatbox': all the brown-felt-hatted Oxenford girls coming from exactly the same kind of family – large house down a long Scottish drive with matching lodges at the gates, a visitors' book in the hall, a stable block, gardeners speaking with Scottish accents and girls definitely speaking with English ones. But it's far from the case that all boarding-school girls came from exactly 'the same hatbox'.

Part of the choosing of a suitable school for the daughter involved an acute parental awareness of subtle differences in the social class of girls that different private schools attracted: for example, the subtle but vital social difference between 'East Coast Scottish families' and 'Glasgow shipping families'. At least three of the grander people I've interviewed have said to me, 'I don't think I've ever met *anyone* who went to Roedean.' When Henry Villiers (father of ex-Cobham Hall daughters) said that to me, his wife added, wryly, 'and that says it all'. About Roedean? About her husband? Perhaps about both.

Henry Villiers cheerfully admitted to having chosen Cobham Hall in the 1970s entirely for its architecture (it's in a beautiful Elizabethan house in Kent), and for the fact that daughters of his friends were going there, so he knew they would make suitable friends. What he dreaded was a 'localized' school; i.e. one 'where all the girls were things like the daughter of the local solicitor in Gravesend'. As for the education, 'I knew that would take care of itself. And, you know, it did.'

'Why on earth did your parents send you there?' was a question I asked my interviewees – and I asked it with more and more head-shaking surprise, the more I heard about life at some of the schools. Here is a selection of the answers I received. Some of the parental reasons were just eccentric; others were actively blinkered and misguided.

First, there was the health reason. 'My parents chose Wycombe Abbey because it was the nearest girls' boarding-school to Harley Street.' (So said Judy England.) Parents like hers were part of the old-style health brigade. Whereas today's health-obsessed parents fret about their children eating organic school food, sixty years ago parents were worried about their children actually dying in an epidemic – and there were frequent epidemics at boarding-schools. For example, when Dormy House at St Enodoc in Cornwall reopened as a hotel in September 1945, the first guests were alarmed to find the place still dotted about with evacuated Portsdown Lodge schoolgirls, languishing in the sickroom or convalescing on chairs in the garden at the tail end of the most recent measles epidemic.

Ensuring that their two daughters were being educated near to the best private doctors in Harley Street wasn't as crazy a priority for Judy's parents as all that. Every parent was haunted by the image of Helen Burns dying at Lowood in *Jane Eyre*. What didn't occur to parents was that one's daughter could emerge from a well-drained, invigorating school extremely physically healthy but with her front teeth knocked out or a nose misshapen from playing lacrosse – as well as chilblained fingers. As it happened, Judy's sister got acute appendicitis while staying with a Wycombe Abbey friend in Bristol during the holidays – well out of reach of emergency treatment in Harley Street.

Then there were the frivolous reasons: 'Daddy thought Hatherop was fun – he thought all the girls looked rather heavenly and pretty' (Lizie de la Morinière). 'My parents chose Heathfield because none of the girls had spots' (Camilla Geffen). 'I think my father rather fancied the headmistress. He was a bit of a ladies' man' (Bolla Denehy). There was a great deal of look-ism going on in these 1950s and '60s choices: both architectural look-ism and facial-features look-ism. 'I want my daughter to look like one of these pretty girls,' fathers decided, as they were given the tour by the blushing headmistress starved of male company.

Sometimes, mothers made snap decisions on a whim: 'My mother went to West Heath for tea once, for some-one's confirmation, and she sent me there entirely on the strength of that nice tea' (Laura Lonsdale). 'Mummy had two prospectuses: for Heathfield and St James's. St James's had a swimming-pool but Heathfield didn't. Heathfield had a tuck shop and St James's didn't. She turned down Heathfield for those two reasons' (Fiona Buchanan). Here we recognize all too well the kind of on-the-spot decisions adults are prone to make – decisions that have a huge impact on the lives of their offspring. It can be something as small as the quality of a toasted teacake that clinches a child's future prospects. By the time Fiona Buchanan and her sister Margaret arrived at the tuck-shopless St James's, the once-great Miss Alice Baird was very old and doddery and was still censoring the letters home.

Then there was the 'Who is my daughter going to be friends with for the rest of her life?' concern: 'My parents wanted me to broaden my outlook, to meet more Londony people' (Fiona Wright, who came down to West Heath in Kent by train from Scotland in 1950). 'My father wanted me to widen my friendships, not just be friends with local farmers' children' (Gigi Richardson, Hanford School,

1970s.) There was a dread of social isolation: somehow parents had to ensure that their daughter would find her way on to a rung of the ladder that would eventually include her in all the best parties and lead her to a suitable marriage. Being closer to London and mingling with the 'right' kind of girls from all over the British Isles, they thought, would help with this.

There were geographical reasons, some sensible, some wishful: 'Hatherop was chosen because it was halfway between London and Cornwall, where my father lived. But he only ever visited me once' (Juliet Mount Charles). This illustrates the adult human tendency not to know ourselves very well. Juliet's father had a vague, optimistic vision that he would be popping in to Hatherop every now and then to see his daughter, but it bore no resemblance to reality, in which out of sight was out of mind. She told me that 'the Irish contingent' chose Hatherop because it was near Cheltenham racecourse. This would only have been of use to the parents on the rare occasions when they bothered to visit their daughters.

Parents sometimes spotted something charming in the prospectus: 'My parents liked St Mary's, Wantage, because the school did weaving,' said Judith Keppel. 'There was a large room full of looms, run by Miss Wimperis, the art mistress. They thought that made it a slightly *different* school. But actually I didn't do weaving in the end.' This is a case of parents not thinking hard about their daughter's preferences.

In spite of (or perhaps because of) its plentiful looms, St Mary's, Wantage in 1955 was not the ideal place to send the young egghead Judith. 'I failed Maths O-level twice and eventually passed on the third go. St Mary's aspired; it was not a hopeless school, but it somehow dulled the spirit and oppressed one.'

What's more, in a school run by Anglican nuns, Judith was terrified of getting 'The Call'. 'We all knew about the previous headmistress, Sister Mary Patricia, who had been young and pretty with a life of fun ahead of her – and The Call came to her like a thunderbolt. She couldn't escape it. She went twice round the world to try to escape it, but to no avail. To me, that was a fate worse than death.'

An unusual reason was to do with the sewing of knickers: 'One of the reasons my mother chose Woldingham was because I'd be with nuns and learn to sew my own underwear' (Victoria Mather). Victoria's mother approved of underwear with the label 'Sewn by nuns in Italy' and imagined her daughter acquiring this useful skill as well as all the other necessary feminine and Catholic accomplishments. 'I was rotten at needlework,' Victoria told me. 'It took me a whole school year to make a baby's dress. My husband wanted to put a sewing machine on our wedding list and I said, "No! Absolutely not."'

There was the father's abhorrence of bad discipline: 'My parents toyed with sending me to the local day school in Sudbury,' said Gillian Darley. 'We went to look round, and the headmaster knocked on a classroom door. "Open up, boys!" he shouted. Nothing happened. My father thought, "There's no discipline here!" and on that basis alone they decided to send me to Riddlesworth Hall.' That was another example of a snap decision, but one based on an instant violent reaction against the alternative.

Three Old Girls told me three contrasting reasons for their having been sent to St Elphin's, Darley Dale. I'd never heard of St Elphin's until I started researching this book and met Emma Tennant, daughter of the late Dowager Duchess of Devonshire, who sent me a photocopy of a page from her 1950s album depicting life at St Elphin's, to which she went as a daygirl from Chatsworth, driven there and back every day by the chauffeur. One of the photographs depicts a tug-of-war between the clergy fathers, in full clerical dress, and the laity fathers, watched by an enthusiastic crowd including the headmistress Miss Stopford or 'Stoppo', the local Dean (Dean Bean, known as 'Dean Seldom Seen'), the Duchess of Devonshire and John Betjeman, family friend of the Cavendishes.

'My mother didn't really believe in education for women,' Emma said. 'She believed "A woman's place is in the home". She herself only ever went to school for three weeks, and she cried all the time. Her parents took her away; then she had a governess who just taught her racing demon; she left; and the next one just taught her shoplifting.'

But Deborah Devonshire was willing to send her education-hungry daughter Emma to the nearby St Elphin's for five years, from 10 to 15, and was always happy to turn up as Guest of Honour at school speech days, to lend tone to the occasion.

Then I met Sharon McVeigh and Pippa Allen, who went to St Elphin's a decade later, in the 1960s and early '70s. Sharon went there because she failed the 11-plus, and it was either that or the Secondary Modern in Buxton. Pippa was sent there because 'it was an aspirational thing. My parents were nouveau-riche, in manufacturing, and it was the done thing to send children to board: that was what you did if you could afford it. Our parents were quite happy to get us out of their hair, and I didn't miss them one iota.'

On these often precarious foundations, having no idea what they were being let in for, but full of hope, girls packed their trunks ('bedjacket' and 'umbrella' were two items on the St James's clothes list) and made their way to the chosen establishment. But what would it be like on the first night and in the first week? As one girl wrote anonymously in the questionnaire devised by Mallory Wober for his 1971 social survey *Girls' Boarding Schools*, 'I have read stories about girls' boarding schools and they are nothing like what it is here.'

2

The New Girl's Surprise

By adulthood we have learned this: places are different from how we expect them to be, and usually a little bit worse. As we approach (say) a rented holiday house in Italy, we savour for the last time our imagined vision of it, because we know that vision will be obliterated by the truth any minute now. We picture the shady terrace with the table laid for breakfast, the vines dripping with grapes and the ravishing view, as shown in the brochure; but we're privately aware that there's probably going to be a poky kitchen, a hob that doesn't work and a smell of drains. We've learned to brace ourselves for this, and anyway, we can always open a good bottle of wine to soften the blow.

Children have more vivid imaginations than grown-ups, and they have no such preparatory mechanism, especially if they've spent years curled up reading *Second Form at Malory Towers*, *The Best of All Schools* and *The Jolliest Term on Record*. For boarding-school new arrivals, there's nothing to soften the blow of reality apart from very soft macaroni cheese for supper.

Girls in their legions, with hats on and hearts pumping, have arrived at their new boarding-schools bursting with excitement and hope. Because it looked like a stately home in the photograph they were shown by their parents, they'd thought they were really going to be living in a stately home: that they would soon be rushing through the panelled hall and out of the French windows of the drawing-room into the garden with all their new friends.

But it was not to be. For a start, entrance was through the back door, not the front door. One of the first things my interviewees learned, on arrival at the actual school and as soon as their parents drove away, was that no pupil went up the main stairs. The beautiful, beckoning, curvy-banistered staircase in the pot-pourri-scented hall of the main house, with its deep-ticking grandfather clock – this was not only out of bounds but rarely even glimpsed.

Miss Di Baird, sister of Miss Alice, used to say tactfully to naïve new girls who were about to rush up the main staircase at St James's, 'That staircase is very *slippery*; the girls always use the other one.' The great houses so cleverly acquired by the indomitable foundresses of the 1890s and 1900s always had at least three staircases, leaving two flights of back stairs for the girls – to walk up, never to run.

For many young girls on the first night it was the back-stairs, lino-floor, vicious-matron shock that gripped their hearts with a cold hand and made them realize that the talk of 'homeliness' had been a con. The Sibton Park prospectus had shown an enticing photograph of girls in kilts sitting cosily by a log fire chatting to the headmistress in the Long Room. The Long Room was a famously beautiful real room of the real house, with a fireplace at each end and Persian rugs on the floor. I hardly went in there, except once or twice when there were power-cuts during the Three-Day Week and we were at last allowed to spend an evening by the Long Room fire. Old Girls who were at Hanford School in Dorset have the same memory: the Three-Day Week was when 'the prospectus came true'.

Perhaps this back-stairs, lino-floor life wasn't so bad, oddly enough, for girls who really had been brought up in stately homes: such girls were used to living in a draughty nursery wing with Nanny, eating lukewarm boiled chicken sent up from a distant kitchen, and only visiting the drawing-room in their best frocks once a day. But for middle-class girls and 'sausage-makers' daughters' – another snooty expression I've heard to sum up a boarding-school 'type' – brought up by stay-at-home mothers in carpeted houses, the sense of exile from the family side of the house was a shock.

Lying on the sagging mattress in the dormitory on their first night, listening to the worldly chat around them, new girls lay rigid with fear about saying the right thing, doing the right thing, being liked and being normal. Far from the jollity of the first evening in an Angela Brazil novel, this was a chilling, lonely few hours. In school stories, girls were celebrated for their different character traits and their eccentric, lovable ways. In non-fiction boarding-schools, it turned out, all you longed for in those first few days was to be exactly the same as everyone else: not to stick out in any way.

Non-fiction boarding-schools, unlike the one in *The Manor House School*, had a warren of under-decorated dormitories on dimly lit corridors along which a really nasty matron prowled, hissing 'How DARE you!' You were allowed exactly two photographs in a frame on the chest of drawers, and one 'soft toy'. It took a brave girl to risk bringing a six-sided photo-cube.

In the strict world of boarding prep-schools, girls caught talking after lights-out were made to sit on the landings in silence for an hour or more, facing the wall.

Morsie was the old governess of Mrs Fyfe's family, and she had been the matron at Hatherop Castle for many decades. By the 1970s, very old indeed, she had long since stopped working and was in a nursing-home. On one of the dark and creaking landings at Hatherop called the Red Landing, Morsie's old china doll was kept in a glass case. New girls were told, on the evening of their arrival, that at the very moment when Morsie died, the doll would break out of its glass case and kill the first girl it saw. It was to the floor in front of this glass case that girls caught talking after lights-out were made to drag their mattresses and spend the night as a punishment. New girls had to get used to the howling and sobbing of these punished girls who were frightened half to death that this would be the night that Morsie's doll would break out.

If not actual initiation ceremonies, there were initiation rituals, and they were mostly enacted in the dark. Anne Heseltine, in bed after lights-out on her first night at St Helen's, Northwood in 1947, had a jug of cold water poured over her. 'I was cold all night. I'd done nothing apart from being a new girl.' On her first night at Cobham Hall, Camilla Cotterell had a tub of talcum powder squirted over her face. (She did become best friends with the girl who squirted it.) On her first night at Castle Howard in 1945 (to which Queen Margaret's, York was evacuated and would be until 1950), Angela Mackenzie was subjected to a weird experience in the moonlight: 'Outside, in the field, the other girls stripped off all your clothes and pummelled you. I remember the other new girl being profoundly upset by this. I thought, the quieter I am, the sooner they'll get it over with.'

'A host of rules came into force,' wrote the St James's, West Malvern, pioneer. How true this is about rules in female establishments! Anyone who has ever compared a convent with a monastery will have noticed that women tend to make more rules than men. Compare the way the genial monks at the Community of the Resurrection at Mirfield wolf down their supper and chat (they pronounce 'pizza' as 'pitzer'), while the West Mailing nuns nibble their bread and marge in silence. It's something to do with tidiness and control: women who run institutions feel the need to keep the lid on the crazy, mad, hormonal world by hemming their charges about with strict rules and even stricter bye-rules.

New girls had to learn all these rules within hours of arrival, and soon discovered that ignorance was no excuse in the eyes of the rule-makers. Shaking with nerves on the first morning, you had to fold the eiderdown, top blanket, bottom blanket, top sheet, bottom sheet and underblanket, in that order, and with the right number of folds, on to the chair beside your bed. Some of my interviewees then also had to arch the lumpy mattress up into a huge tunnel shape, to air it properly. After breakfast, you had to reassemble these elements, and many boarding-school girls have been slightly obsessed with hospital corners ever since. They can't pass a bed in any school, house or indeed hospital without checking the sheets have been tucked in properly.

Then, in the new environment, you had to get used to your days for washing. For baths, you might be either a Monday, Wednesday and Friday person or a Tuesday, Thursday and Saturday person. So powerful were the auras of these allocated bath-days that for the rest of their lives, boarding-school girls feel they belong in one of two camps. For half the population, Monday, Wednesday and Friday are primary-coloured days while Tuesdays, Thursdays and Saturdays are beige.

Hair-washing was rarer: once a fortnight, and (at some schools) not at all if you had your period. Quite what the connection was, no one knew, but it made a good excuse for those who didn't like hair-washes. At Sibton Park, Matron plunged your head into a basin and scrubbed vigorously with her squeaky rubber gloves on. Then you had to towel-dry your hair with aching arms until it was almost dry: only then were you allowed two minutes by the blow-heater.

At St Leonards, for many decades from before the war to the late 1960s, the girls had the same visiting man, known as Hairy Man, to wash their hair. A friendly man with dark Brylcreamed hair, he worked in the local salon in St Andrews and went round each boarding-house, washing each girl's hair in a basin with industrial shampoo from a gallon-sized container. No girl was allowed to wash her own hair. 'People sometimes did,' remembers Vicky Peterkin who was there in the 1950s, 'but it was obvious they had done so as they had gone to bed with wet hair and it had dried into an unruly mop in the morning.'

There was another man, Bug Man, who came at the beginning of each term to check the girls for nits. Also, in your first week at St Leonards, you had to endure the ordeal of 'house backs'. This entailed stripping down to your knickers and standing facing the wall while the games mistress examined your posture. There were three possible diagnoses: 'round shoulders', 'squint shoulders' and 'flat feet'. Each condition required extra drill in the gymnasium each morning between morning prep and prayers: hanging from a bar with both hands for 'round shoulders', or hanging just with one hand for 'squint'.

Girls who had been innocently going about their personal health and hygiene at home had to get used to this new timetabled and rule-bound routine. Who would have dreamed there would be rules and sub-rules about tooth-brushing? At Sibton Park you had to get half-changed, then brush your teeth in your vest and pants, and then finish the job of getting changed. This was to avoid toothpaste spillage but that was not explained. At Woldingham in Surrey, in the 1960s, you had to wash with a bowl of soapy water and then use the same water to brush your teeth. Markie Robson-Scott was brushing her teeth on her first evening at Badminton School in 1961 when the Junior House matron, Miss Cryer, barked at her, 'You're brushing your teeth wrong. Are you an only child?'

Markie was indeed an only child; but what was it about the way she brushed her teeth that had caused Miss Cryer to make this Sherlock-Holmesian deduction?

'It wasn't so much about the brushing as about the rinsing,' Markie explained to me. 'I think I spat the water back into the tooth-mug or something. No one had ever told me not to at home. From the moment Miss Cryer said those words I started thinking my parents were odd, and realized that I didn't come from a normal family. Suddenly I didn't trust my parents' judgements any more. It was devastating.'

*

This longing to conform, to be seamlessly absorbed into the crowd and not stand out, seems universal. All too often it was the thoughtless parents who caused their children to veer from normality. Pippa Allen's father worked in textiles, and for Pippa's St Elphin's, Darley Dale uniform 'he got a bolt of worsted in not quite the right colour – very good quality, though'.

'I remember it!' said Sharon MacVeigh. 'It was a bit shinier than it was meant to be.'

'*Very* embarrassing.'

Artemis Cooper's mother bought her the wrong-sized shoes, for Woldingham in the 1950s. 'Absolute clodhoppers, three sizes too large. Everyone else had dainty shoes from Clarks.'

'My thrifty mother', said Linda Cubitt (Southover in the 1940s), 'got me a skirt with a bodice. No one else had a bodice.'

'I had a straight skirt on my afternoon frock,' said Mary James (St Leonards, late 1950s, and later to become headmistress of that same school). 'No one else had a straight skirt.'

'Our parents never gave us the right uniform,' said Georgina Hammick (Beaufront, 1950). 'Our mother had cut the pleats out of our tweed skirts so we could hardly walk. In the evening we had to wear red dresses with Peter Pan collars: I had a grey one. My twin sister Amanda had a red one but it had puffed sleeves. Why couldn't we have had the right clothes?'

These girls spent their first week acutely self-conscious,

plodding about in their huge shoes or shuffling about in their too-straight skirts, feeling like aliens.

Adding to the trauma of sartorial differentness was the awkwardness of arriving in the middle of a school year. This was a recurring theme and it always made life twice as lonely for a new girl. Judith Kerr, born in 1923 and my oldest interviewee, went to Hayes Court in Kent in January 1938. 'It was odd to arrive in the middle of the year,' Judith said, talking to me in her house in Barnes where she had prepared coffee in a kitchen that reminded me of the one in her book *The Tiger Who Came to Tea*. 'One was totally *visible*. It didn't help that I was dressed in the hand-me-down uniform of a girl who had just left, who had been very unpopular.'

The Kerr family had left Germany in 1933, and for two years Judith and her brother had lived with their grandparents in Nice. 'My grandmother was keen on us learning English and took us to the English library in Nice, where there was a whole corner devoted to Angela Brazil. I picked my way through them all with the help of a dictionary. So I thought boarding-school was going to be terrific and when I arrived at Hayes Court I said everything was "topping" and "ripping". Everyone laughed at me.'

In London Judith and her impoverished parents had no fixed abode. Her father, a scriptwriter and drama critic, had sold a script to Alexander Korda, really a gesture of kindness on Korda's part as he had no intention of making the film.

'We lived for two years in a shabby hotel in Bloomsbury, and I did lessons with some American girls who were learning at home. Then my parents fell on even harder times. Various extraordinarily kind people got my mother a job as social secretary to Lady Wimborne, which she hated, but it did help. These friends paid for my brother to go to a public school, Aidenham, which was a huge success, and the school showered him with scholarships when my parents could no longer pay. I was more of a problem.'

With the kindest of motives, the English friends of Judith's parents clubbed together to send her to Hayes Court. Years later Judith saw a letter her father had written to her mother, questioning whether this was the right course of action for their daughter: '"Please don't send Judith there as she's sure to be humiliated." He saw that I was going as a wildly impoverished child into this rich milieu.'

Sure enough, things did not go well. 'The school play was *The Merchant of Venice*, and as it was vaguely known that my father was a drama critic, I was given the part of Nerissa. The director of the play was the young Alec Guinness – his future wife was designing the costumes. The girl who was playing Portia was really keen on acting, and she was not at all pleased when Alec Guinness's friend, who wrote a review of the play, didn't write about Portia at all but wrote all about Nerissa.'

This unforgivable perceived limelight-stealing, and the wearing of the hand-me-down unpopular girl's dress, and the misuse of dated Angela Brazil schoolgirl slang, and

arriving in the middle of the school year, all counted against
Judith. 'Hands up who hasn't got a partner,' said the dancing mistress, and it was always her.

Two girls said to her, 'Did your nanny have a Cockney
accent?' Judith wasn't sure how to answer this. In Germany
they'd had Heimpi, who had done the cooking and the
sewing. 'I don't know,' she said; 'Why do you ask?' 'Because
we've all been discussing it and we've decided your vowels
aren't pure.'

The crowning awkwardness of those first two terms was
that Judith had to be seen to be deeply grateful to the gen-
erous people who were paying for her to go there. In letters
home she had to say she was having a lovely time.

Over the summer holidays she wiped the school from
her memory. 'When term began in September 1939, I'd
forgotten everyone's names. I'd even forgotten the name of
the games captain. She roared with laughter and from that
moment on I became known as a sort of eccentric.'

That term, she made friends with Lavinia Thorpe, who
had played Shylock. Lavinia was truly kind and not a snob.
'Everyone else went out to lunch at the local county hotel in
their parents' cars,' Judith said. 'My parents always came to
visit me on the Green Line bus and we went out to the local
Mary and John's tea-shop in the village. We took Lavinia
out to tea with us there, and when *her* parents came to take
us out to tea, she insisted on going not to the county hotel
but to Mary and John's tea-shop.'

*

Here we see a common boarding-school progression: first, loneliness, unpopularity and a terrible sense of being different from everyone else; then, becoming famous for being some kind of eccentric or clown; then, making a real friend, which made life bearable. But no girl ever forgets those chilling words: 'We've all been discussing it.' They speak of a whole social world going on behind the new girl's lonely, unpopular, alien, excluded back.

But who was supervising all this? Who, exactly, was '*in loco parentis*', and was she at all parent-like? Generally, she was Miss someone.

3

The Misses

The title 'Miss' in the plural has all but vanished from current usage. It was common in the days when unmarried sisters ran schools together. When you read, in the 1935 Truman & Knightley Schools Directory, that Netherhall School in Bournemouth was run by 'the Misses Stevens', Bartrum Gables in Broadstairs by 'Miss Winifred M. Crittall and Miss E. Olive Crittall', and 'The Chilterns' in Buckinghamshire by 'Mrs G. L. Moore and Miss Ilma Moore', whole poignant imagined life-stories come to mind: the pairs of spinster sisters who would surely have married if a generation of young men hadn't been killed in the First World War; the widowed mother needing to find some way for her and her daughter to scratch a living; the flatness of having to live out long desiccated lives in almost exclusively same-sex company. No wonder these women flirted with the occasional visiting father.

Just as intriguing as the pairs of women with the same surnames are the pairs with different ones: Chantry Mount in Bishop's Stortford run by 'Miss N. Harries and Miss G. M. Fisher' or The Laurels in Rugby by 'Miss Jolly and Miss Rutter'. With our modern awareness we can't resist the thought, 'Were they lesbians?' The truth is, we shall never know, and some of them probably were. I've lost count of the number of times my interviewees have said to me, 'With hindsight I suppose they must have been lesbians, but of course, we hadn't even heard the word in those days.'

Occasionally a girl caught a glimpse in the dead of night of a schoolmistress, in a lacy nightdress and with her hair down, slipping into the bedroom of another mistress, and these glimpses left lasting impressions. One girl remembered being told off for talking after lights-out, first by the matron and then, five minutes later, by the housemistress, both of them wearing the selfsame pink velour dressing-gown. Going to say the obligatory 'goodnight' to the housemistress Miss Dyer at the evacuated Queen Margaret's, York in 1947, Angela Mackenzie found the housemistress sitting on her sofa with the domestic-science mistress on the floor beside her, cuddling up to her knees.

'I was so flummoxed that I got their names twisted,' said Angela. 'Miss Dyer looked lovingly down at the domestic-science mistress and said, "It's all the same to us, isn't it?"' Patricia Daunt mentioned in passing, in her vivacious recollections of Southover Manor School, Lewes in the 1950s, that the headmistress Miss Aspden's girlfriend was the school secretary, the French mistress was in love with the games mistress, and the English mistress was in love with the scripture mistress. But my interviewees have stressed that girls' boarding-school staff wings were not necessarily hotbeds. Many beds were decidedly cold, narrow and occupied by single women.

'What was her life really like?' you can't help wondering, when you look at the thin-haired headmistress in a buttoned-up cardie and string of pearls, sitting straight-backed in the middle of the front row of a girls' boarding-school photograph of the 1930s, '40s or '50s. You think of her bedroom in the corridor of single rooms in the staff wing, each with its hissing gas fire, and the long empty holidays looming.

'I think Miss Walker is not the only one who experiences stage fright when the curtain is just going to rise on a new term,' wrote Miss Alice Baird, with her customary sense of excitement, reminding us that these schoolmistresses did have lives in the holidays but that these were thin affairs compared to the richness of life in term-time. Were these unmarried women merely the back-stage crew of the real drama, which was the girls? I think in many cases they were, and that some of them loved this existence and some found it difficult. The ones who loved it could be selfless and inspiring women who devoted their lives to their school and to their girls, and instilled a similar sense of selflessness in their pupils. The ones who found it difficult sometimes took their frustration and embitterment out on unsuspecting new girls.

Describing these women, my interviewees have tended to make one of two gestures with their hands: either 'bosoms out to here', or 'bosoms down to here'. I've been wondering which is preferable. 'Bosoms out to here' implies stoutness, a certain majesty, a trip to a lingerie department once a year for a bigger cup-size, a lifetime of comfort-eating of stodgy school puddings, an increasing difficulty in getting in and out of the bath, a ship-like presence in the corridors. 'Bosoms down to here' implies dowdiness, thinness, a gradual sagging of breasts and self-esteem induced by a lifetime of all-female company, a cycle of lack of vanity leading to never buying any new underwear, leading to even less vanity. I think perhaps 'bosoms down to here' is worse.

Miss Blewett and Miss Griesbach, both excellent and kind teachers who ran the evacuated Portsdown Lodge during the war, were the 'out-to-here' kind. 'Both had formidable shelf-like bosoms,' remembers Josephine Boyle, 'and they appeared to glide around the school on impossibly small feet.' Miss Gray, the head matron at Heathfield in the 1970s likewise had 'bosoms out to here', remembered the Heathfield Old Girls I spoke to; 'She had a loud, strong voice and knocked girls over like skittles to get to the one who was talking.'

'Jellybags' at Southover in the 1950s had the 'down-to-here' kind: 'Jellybags taught us English,' said Vicky

Whitworth: 'bosoms down to her waist, and she had a beard.' To listen to Old Girls reminiscing about their boarding-school headmistresses and teachers is to build up a gallery of extraordinary-looking women – bosomy, bearded, whiskered, wizened, grunting, sometimes all at once – and one can only wonder how crestfallen the mistresses in question would have been if they'd heard themselves described in this way – especially the down-to-here ones. Crestfallen *and* breast-fallen.

The nicknames given to mistresses never made their names any prettier. They were unoriginal and obvious: the first that came to someone's mind and stuck. Any Miss Turner was 'The Turnip'. Any Miss Pollard was 'Polly'. Miss Aspden was 'The Asp', Miss Reynolds 'The Wren', and Miss Bullock 'The Bull'. At St James's the matron Miss Dare was 'Devil Dare', and the Maths teacher Wendy Bates was 'Bendy Weights'. Deaconess Mirch, who ran St Helen's, Northwood's Mission in Islington, was 'Deaconess Smirch'. Lady Eglinton, who ran Oxenford, was 'The Egg'. The use of the definite article has the effect of turning these characters from women into exhibits.

Some of them looked like men. The headmistress of St Felix, Southwold in the 1960s, Mary Oakley ('Moak'), looked like Henry VIII, with the same broad face, standing position and clothing shape. 'She taught very basic history,' said Tanya Harrod. 'She came from a military family and had conventional views. In the final year you went to her drawing-room once a week and you got a blast of her prejudices, such as that black people smelled different. If you were cool, you tried to be out of her sightlines.'

Miss Belshaw (known as 'Belly'), who ran the girls' prep-school Leelands in Kent, wore 'a hat like a Stetson', remembers Liz Forgan, 'and had hairs coming out of her chin'. For decades she ran the school with Miss Taylor ('Tay'), 'a sweet lady with a limp, who used to read *The Wind in the Willows* to us in the Quiet Room'. Miss Waters at Southover in the early 1950s taught Maths in a guttural German accent – 'we thought she was not just a spy but a *male* spy', remembered three Old Southover Girls, Cecilia Neal, Linda Cubitt and Cynthia Colman. 'We threw our pencil-sharpeners on to the floor on purpose just so we could pick them up and have a glimpse up her skirt, to check.'

Even today, if a child spots a schoolteacher out of context, such as in a hairdressing salon on Easter Monday, the sight comes as a comic surprise. ('I saw her in the hairdresser's! Can you believe it!') In the mid-twentieth century there was even more of a chasm between pupils and their superiors. It hardly occurred to girls that their schoolmistresses had private lives and certainly not that they had ever had or could ever have loves of their own. Resident unmarried boarding-school mistresses were simply a feature of life; towns on the south coast were thickly populated with them, and the girls hardly gave a thought to what might be going on in their hearts and souls.

*

Once, on a summer evening at Sibton Park in 1974, four girls including me sat in our dormitory and sang 'In Dublin's Fair City' to Miss Brunning.

She died of a fever,
And no one could save her,
And that was the end of sweet Molly Malone ...

I looked up and noticed that Miss Brunning was silently sobbing, in the way that only a very disciplined old lady can: with controlled, stifled, heaving sobs. I've never forgotten it. It had never occurred to me that Miss Brunning or indeed any of the Misses I had ever come across could cry. Was this the pent-up sadness of a long, lonely life gushing to the fore? Or was it just the normal tearfulness of any middle-aged woman on hearing children blithely singing a folksong with no real understanding of the levels of tragedy described?

Markie Robson-Scott remembers a similar episode at Badminton in 1961. 'All the teachers were spinsters with Robin Hood fringes. The matron in our house, Phoebe Starr, was very strange. She would strip the bed with you in it. She would come in when you were in the bath. I think she was probably a very sad person. I think she liked me. One day she invited me into her bedroom – it was really warm, with a gas fire, unlike our cold dorm. She said to me, "You know, people don't like *rude girls*." It was a kind of pep-talk on how to behave. Then she started to cry.'

Miss Furnival, the violin teacher at Queen Margaret's, York

used to go into the garden at lunch time to talk to the flowers: another sign of loneliness leading to a kind of madness.

Miss Flint at Wycombe Abbey didn't cry, but she did ask her girls to analyse 'Smoke Gets in Your Eyes' for its imagery, which made them wonder: did she have a romantic side? She was a meticulous, perfectionist English teacher who hardly ever gave any girl an 'A', and when talking about Shakespeare preferred to explain the precise meaning of the lines rather than dwell on their magic and beauty. I've studied her photograph on the dust-jacket of *Wycombe Abbey: A Partial History* and she looks like any other schoolmistress of the 1950s – brisk, buttoned-up, keeping her smile well under control.

But, as the Wycombe Abbey girls I interviewed at Cicely Taylor's flat in Notting Hill remembered, she was the one teacher who *didn't* wear the same clothes every single day. 'The teachers were conspicuously poor. One was aware that they were wearing the same tweed suit all year – apart from Miss Flint. She borrowed clothes from her sister who lived in Birmingham. We kept a record of what she wore: during her English lessons, we wrote it down.'

'There was a merriment in Miss Flint's features,' remembers Fiona MacCarthy. 'Her sister, who sometimes used to come to school to help out with Shakespeare productions, was more gaunt. She didn't go in for pussy-cat bows round her neck as *our* Miss Flint did. We used to speculate about whether she'd lost a fiancé in the war.'

The person Miss Flint was really in love with was

Shakespeare. Her *Partial History* is sprinkled all over with Shakespeare quotes woven into her sentences. 'There's a divinity that shapes our ends – the quotation is as apt as it is irresistible . . . ' and (at the end of the acknowledgements), such-and-such are 'my only reasons for regret at having reached the end of this particular love's labour'. When the young Fiona MacCarthy (inspired by reading Kenneth Tynan's fashionably sharp reviews) dared to write a scathing review of Laurence Olivier and Vivien Leigh's *Macbeth*, Miss Flint was distinctly displeased.

'The Wycombe Abbey housemistresses were a bizarre bunch,' said Anne Barnes, who was there in the early 1950s. 'We didn't realize how bizarre they were: elderly women who'd had no experience of husbands or children. Miss Clare had an absolute clinch on her favourites, to whom she could be nasty as well as nice. Her car was her real partner: a little rusty car. She used to drive it like a lunatic round and round the drive.' Meanwhile the muscular Latin teacher Miss Pollard 'roared at us', remembers Michaela Reid. 'Polly was in love with Caesar. We were so terrified of her tests that we learned by torchlight.'

You get the sense, from these descriptions, of women burning with repressed emotion: one in love with Shakespeare, one with Caesar, and one with her car, all of them living out their lives in the confines of a same-sex school. They had to let their emotions out somehow. When they contemplated their infinite future in the same establishment, it must sometimes have seemed bleak indeed. The French teacher

Miss Pettiward at Cranborne Chase in Dorset was 'always stitching', remembers Caroline Cranbrook. 'What are you making?' the girls asked her. 'It's my shroud,' she replied.

In boys' prep-schools during and just after the war it was perhaps worse: the best masters had gone off to fight, leaving the less adequate ones to be headmasters of boys' prep-schools, as Josephine Boyle's husband Humphrey remembers all too well from Charney Hall in Cumbria, where both the headmaster and his wife were 'sozzled by 5 p.m.', and another master was found taking lead off the church roof. Girls' schools didn't suffer from the same brain drain, but there could still be a pall of gloom emanating from women whose careers and love-lives had reached a cul-de-sac.

'Miss, Miss, Miss, Miss, Miss, Miss ... ' If you scroll down the vast staff list from Cheltenham Ladies' College in the early 1950s, you go a long way before you come to a single 'Mrs', let alone a man. The man was Dr Herbert Sumsion, director of music and well-known composer. My ears pricked up when Georgina Hammick told me she had had an excellent English teacher at Beaufront called Mr Butts. It turned out it was not Mr Butts but Miss De Butts. The cook at Beaufront was known as Mrs Todd, but the 'Mrs' was honorary: she was a single woman but 'Mrs' sounded right for a cook. Very occasionally a Miss would genuinely become a Mrs, or do even better. The music mistress at St Helen's, Northwood in the early 1950s went on a Swan Hellenic cruise to convalesce from an illness. On board she made friends with one of the lecturers and on her return invited him to come and give a lecture to the school. A day or two after the lecture the headmistress, Miss Mackenzie, announced to the girls: 'Next term Miss Wilmot will be known as Lady Shelley.'

The excitement! Rags to riches! Or, at least, the same tweed skirt to a wide variety of tweed skirts. The girls thought Miss Mackenzie's announcement a prissy way of announcing a forthcoming wedding, and anyway it came as no surprise: they had spotted Miss Wilmot helping Sir James to repack his suitcase.

Miss Creed and Miss Richards, 'Creedie and Richie', ran Beaufront, near Camberley, a school that was detested alike by Sal Rivière, her twin sisters Georgina Hammick and Amanda Vesey, and Mary Villiers, all of whom went there between the mid-'40s and mid-'50s. It had a famously good collection of rhododendrons, and they've loathed rhododendrons ever since. Miss Creed and Miss Richards were 'bosoms-down-to-here' women, both bespectacled and wearing draped cardigans which went down even lower over their enormous bodies. Their shoes had thick rubber soles that made 'a terrible squishing noise' as they prowled the corridors in search of anyone breaking one of the countless petty rules. 'They made you feel', said Sal Rivière, 'that you had left undone those things which you ought to have done, and done those things which you ought not to have done, and that there was no health in you.'

Which is a sign that any Beaufront Old Girl at least knows reams of the *Book of Common Prayer* by heart. 'There was nothing to like about Richie,' said Sal, 'but Creedie taught Scripture and Shakespeare, both of which she did extremely well.'

'Creedie and Richie put up notices every day,' said Georgina Hammick, 'and the notices always began with the words, "All those girls". "All those girls who were seen on the terrace in gym shoes should report to the study at 2 o'clock." This caused fear: had you been one of them? You felt punished all the time.'

When you were summoned to the study, Miss Creed and Miss Richards did not talk directly to you; they talked about you to each other. This was a sinister and powerful tool of belittlement. So, when Amanda was summoned to the study one day, aged 14, and dared to say, 'I looked at the girls coming out of Chapel today, and not a single one was smiling. I think this is a very unhappy school,' there was a moment's silence before Miss Creed said to Miss Richards, 'I don't think Amanda can be feeling quite well, do you, Miss Richards?'

'No, I don't think she can be feeling at all well, Miss Creed. I think the only answer is that she should go to bed at the same time as the early bedders from now on.'

'I agree with you, Miss Richards. She should run upstairs to Matron straight away and tell her she'll be having supper with the early bedders.'

And so it was: 14-year-old Amanda had to go to bed at 6.30 for the rest of the term.

What made things worse was that Creedie and Richie insisted on the girls knowing by heart and lustily singing the much-too-cheerful house songs. They weren't called 'houses', actually, they were called 'patrols'. Girls could be Anchors, Swifts, Greathearts, Diehards or Pioneers. The Swifts' song went:

> *Swifts, remember, never falter,*
> *When the work seems hard to do,*
> *Face it laughing, smiling, singing –*
> *Cheerfulness will see you through.*

Amanda was sent out of class one day. Miss Creed passed her in the corridor and asked her why she had been sent out. 'I was facing it laughing, smiling and singing, Miss Creed,' Amanda replied. She had committed the crime of taking the Swifts' song literally.

Were Miss Richards and Miss Creed sexually frustrated women who were taking their misery out on the girls? According to Sal Rivière they were in fact a happy couple, living cosily together in their own wing, a wing which none of the girls ever saw: the closest you ever came to it was when you had to dispose of your used sanitary towel, wrapped in newspaper, in one of three designated bins round the school, one of which happened to be at the entrance to Creedie and Richie's wing.

As well as being snobbish, the pair had an anti-Semitic streak, so they were doubly nasty to a Jewish girl from London whose father was in the rag-trade. They were far from the only anti-Semitic headmistresses I heard of: there was a lot of it about. Miss Brown, the statuesque headmistress of Queen Margaret's, York during the war, who changed into a long brown evening dress for supper each evening, made life very unhappy for a girl called Pam Hirsch, Angela Mackenzie said, and she was also 'stroppy' with Pam's father. She liked fathers who were in the Anglican Church. 'She liked my father', said Angela, 'because he was vicar of Kippax, and then became Archdeacon of Leeds.'

I've mentioned that girls were not allowed on the main staircase in most girls' boarding-schools. At Beaufront, even the staff weren't allowed on the main stairs. The only two who were permitted to walk up and down the main staircase were Miss Creed and Miss Richards, who went grandly up and down with their great cardigans billowing. The rest of the staff were crammed on to the crowded back stairs. This made them feel undervalued, and they took their frustration out on the girls.

'Twin,' said Mrs Lowther, the exhausted and demoralized geography mistress, to Amanda as she was walking to prep one evening. (Amanda and Georgina were identical twins and were used to being called 'Twin' by the teachers, who couldn't be bothered to work out which was which.) 'Please help me carry my books to my car.'

Amanda duly did so, so she was a minute late for prep. She went into the prep room, and without looking up, Miss Fleming, who was taking prep, said, 'Punctuality mark!'

'But I was helping Mrs Lowther carry her books to the car, Miss Fleming.'

To which Miss Fleming barked, 'Order mark!'

'I felt like Jane Eyre,' said Amanda, who in her late seventies was baking a cake in Wiltshire when I rang her, and we got so caught up in all this that the cake burned. 'The unfairness! They really were rather pathetic people, those women.'

'DW' – Rosemarie Dillon-Weston – taught at Lawnside for thirty years from the 1950s, and Old Girls remember her either with enormous gratitude and affection, if she liked them, or with loathing, if she picked on them. Angela Huth has written persuasively about DW as a wonderful English teacher who helped her towards her writing career. 'We were thrilled by her vision,' she wrote in a piece for the *Daily Mail*. 'She taught us to think for ourselves; to discover, to observe, to feel. For those, like me, who had always intended to write, it was a gift beyond compare.' Rosie de Courcy, on the other hand, burned the manuscript of her novel – a manuscript for which Penguin was begging her in the 1980s – so denuded of confidence was she after having been belittled for years by DW.

So, who was this woman who could raise girls to great heights or knock them down almost to destruction on a whim? She had wanted to become an Oxford don but had

instead become a schoolteacher. 'She came from a large
Bristol family,' Rosie said, 'and I feel that at some point disappointment and bitterness entered into her. There was no
stage for her talents. She felt marginalized. She developed
an icy line in sarcasm.'

'What did she look like?' I asked.

'She wore the same tweed suit every day, and never a bra.
She had her hair in a plait around her head. She wore short
socks and lace-ups, and marched over the Malvern Hills to
school and back to her cottage which she shared with her
sister, whom she bullied.'

She asked the girls in her English class to draw a map of
their minds. 'We had a go at doing this,' Rosie said, 'and
DW ripped into us. "What I see here is the pursuit of happiness. Happiness! Young wenches trying to pursue that
lovely man who will make you happy. You should NEVER
pursue selfish love and happiness. You should pursue goodness, truth, honour and scholarship, but *not* happiness." She
gave us a *pasting*.'

She was brutally scathing about Rosie's taste for the
romantic novels of Georgette Heyer and confiscated them.
(Rosie has taken revenge by becoming Director of Fiction at
the publisher Head of Zeus.) 'She would jeeringly read out
to the class something I'd written.' It was DW who wrote
'cliché, cliché, cliché, cliché, cliché' down the margin of an
essay that Rosie had worked hard on. 'I was terrified of her,
but one day I wrote an essay that I really thought she'd love.
I was desperate to see whether she'd given it a good mark,

so I crept into her office and she caught me searching for it on her desk. She was furious. "You have a bump of anger inside you which you're going to have to master before it masters you," she hissed.'

One day she invited a few of the Sixth Form girls to tea in her cottage, and this gave Rosie a glimpse of her terrifying teacher's mysterious home-life on the other side of the Malverns. 'She was quite patronizing to her sister and called her "Dear". She gave us a gargantuan tea, which she almost force-fed us. There was a sad motherliness about her. She was obsessed with her garden and her cats.'

Mother Ida, the Swiss-born class mistress of the juniors at the Assumption Convent, evacuated from Ramsgate to Herefordshire during the war, had a cruel streak. The evacuated convent was generally a paradise, as we'll see in a later chapter; Mother Ida was the sole fiend. 'She was small and neurotic,' said Catherine Freeman, 'and she made life hell for anyone smaller than her. She was sadistic – she habitually woke up an asthmatic friend of mine, Mary Bowen, by laughingly placing a pillow over her face. You forget how powerless children in boarding-schools were in those days. I did mention to my mother that Mother Ida could be rather cruel, but she said, "Oh, darling, surely the Reverend Mother would *never* allow that."' Mother Ida was very good with her hands, always trying to make things out of spare parts. She got hold of the doll of a friend of Catherine's who was 6 years old, and said, 'Well, I'm sure the poor children in Africa would like this dolly. Now, if I could just take off her *hair*, and her *hands* . . . ' Catherine did wrenching gestures to imitate Mother Ida pulling off the doll's body parts, watched by the distraught 6-year-old.

A speciality of Miss Vernon-Harcourt, headmistress of Runton Hill in Norfolk just after war, was demystifying the Miracles. Another stout disciplinarian with grey hair in a bun, 'Miss Vernon-Harcourt told us,' said Patricia Bergqvist at her house in Buckinghamshire, 'that Lazarus wasn't really dead; that there simply were enough loaves and fishes to go round at the picnic; and that Jesus walking on water was an optical illusion.' All their lives, the girls who were told these things by their headmistress have been as unimpressed by New Testament magic as a too-clever boy watching a conjuror.

Hilda Violet Stuart, headmistress of Sherborne School for Girls in the 1940s, was another 'formidable creature' who walked with what Sally Beazley remembers as 'a hockey stride'. 'If she came along the corridor you had to stand with your back against the wall as she passed.' She had a brother who was a bishop in Uganda so, far from demystifying the Miracles, she taught them as God's own truth. 'If she was crossing a courtyard and we saw her,' said Sally, 'we had to go out and walk with her. She made grunting noises. She didn't say, "Now, how are you?" – she just grunted at you. We were all a bit scared of her.'

*

They were tough, these unmarried women. They themselves had been brought up by strict governesses, and some of them had been girls at the schools they were now teaching at or running. They believed strongly in doing good works. Girls were invited into the housemistress's drawing-room to knit or crochet for charity while the housemistress read aloud to them from an improving book. 'We knitted hot-water-bottle covers for the Melanesians,' said Cicely Taylor. 'As if they needed them!' These drawing-room visits gave girls a glimpse of a prettier, more homely world than the one on their side of the green-baize door.

Some of the Misses were kind; some were intellectuals; some were deadly dull; some were arbiters of good taste and gave girls a lifelong aesthetic sensibility. Some were snobbish, favouring the titled girls and picking on the girls of lower birth. Miss Medley, the tall, elegant headmistress of Downe House near Newbury in the 1950s, was one of the snobbish ones. At the end of Amanda Theunissen's first (and, as it turned out, only) year at Downe House in 1954, Miss Medley said to her, 'I understand your mother runs a café?' To which Amanda replied, 'Yes, she does.' Her mother did run a café, next to Winchester Cathedral Close. 'Of course, we have nothing against *trade*,' said Miss Medley. 'Lady Clay runs a hat-shop. That's *different*, of course.' After this conversation, Miss Medley rang Amanda's mother and suggested her daughter might be happier at Malvern Girls' College. Which she was.

Generally, all the Misses looked ancient, even if they

were only in their forties or early fifties. Actually, most girls positively liked the certainty that these women were never, ever going to be their friends. 'They were ageless and old and sexless, and that's how we liked it,' said Amanda Theunissen. 'One of the reasons why I disliked my housemistress at Malvern was that she did want to be my friend. I didn't *want* to sit in her horrible, highly scented, much-too-warm room and discuss the problems of adolescence. You thought she might hold your hand and stroke it.'

What became of these women? Miss Flint (strict but just and not a snob) retired to the most apt place for her: a cottage in Stratford-upon-Avon round the corner from the theatre, where she lived with her sister, still swapping clothes and going to every Shakespeare production. She was 'completely happy in her Shakespearian haven', said Fiona MacCarthy.

As for the Beaufront pair, Miss Creed was chesty and had asthma and died before Miss Richards. 'Richie retired to North Wales with the matron, Sister Campbell, who was an absolute bitch, actually,' Sal Rivière told me. (That matron had said to Sal's sister Amanda one day, 'If I was your mother, *I'd* live abroad.')

Mother Ida went on to have a complete breakdown – Catherine Freeman found this out because her sister became a nun and knew the secrets of the community. She was sent off to a convent in Denmark and never worked with children again. 'It was because the war was on,' Catherine said, 'that the problem wasn't dealt with.'

Hilda Violet Stuart, as a very old, retired woman, 'wandered around, knitting bootees for Old Girls' babies', remembers Susan Beazley. 'I thought that was rather sad.'

As grown-ups in their forties, Rosie de Courcy and a friend of hers dared to go and visit Miss Dillon-Weston in the 1990s, just before she died. Old DW was still living in the same cottage on the Malverns, now without her sister and without her cats. She was wearing a purple tweed suit with purple socks – 'hideous', said Rosie. 'The incredibly beautiful friend I was with had been one of DW's favourites – she had always given her essays top marks. Not a single thing had changed. She still gazed at my friend with a kind of shy rapture – most unsettling. To me, she was just as vicious as she had always been. I wanted to ask her a bit about herself. I said to her, "We know so little about *your* life. We'd love to know more." She looked at me with savage contempt. I was completely cut down to size, three decades after I'd left the school. I wish I'd probed her more. I wish I'd said, "Why – WHY? What was your problem?"'

Rosie had won an Exhibition to Girton to read English, thanks not to Lawnside but to Cheltenham Technical College, where she did her A-levels, and to Westminster Tutors, where she was crammed for Oxbridge. Did DW at least praise her for this achievement in her own subject when Rosie visited her in the 1990s?

'No, she didn't. She just said, "You should have read Modern Languages."'

DW died alone in her cottage, several days after a fall.

4

Degrees of Separation

Here are some first pages of letters to the 9-year-old Josceline Dimbleby, sent to her at Knighton House school in Dorset by her mother in 1952–3. They are all headed 'British Legation, Damascus' and are written on thick mourning paper after the death of George VI.

Darling Jossy,
I have done such a big drawing, that there is hardly room
for writing on this page! This is written the day before you
go back to school . . .

Darling Jossy,
Here is a new photograph of Matthew, just going to take a
large bite out of a piece of gingerbread!

Darling Jossy,
I hope this letter will be at school to greet you when you
arrive – wishing you a very happy term and lots of fun
and successful work! At the end of this term we shall see
each other again, and it won't seem very long now.
There is a playground here for little children now, and
Matthew . . .

Darling Jossy,
Your letter just arrived while I was doing these drawings!
They seem to come very quickly now: I wonder whether
they come on the 'Comet' which only takes five and a half
hours from London to Beirut.
Matthew often loses his temper now. When he is not
allowed to do something he wants to do, he gives a
loud scream, stamps his foot, and throws himself on the
floor – and . . .

Darling Jossy,
We have got a new official car, and the old Humber is not
used any more. It is an Austen 'Sheerline', very smart with
a wireless set and a heater, but it is not quite as big as the
Humber. I'm afraid there's not room for Matthew's pram
in it. Tomorrow we are going for a picnic to Chamlane up
in the Lebanese mountains to see the Fletchers . . .

These letters are small works of art. The reason there are
so few words on the first pages is that Josceline's mother

had made the 'D' and 'J' of 'Darling Jossy' into exquisite
watercolour garlands of flowers. The thick mourning paper
proved ideal for watercolours. Before starting to write, she
half-filled each first page with paintings of exotic flowers in
vases or leafy branches reaching up to the corners.

Josceline showed me only the first pages; but they were
enough. They reveal so much: the guilt of the mother who
has married a second husband and has had a new baby with
whom she is very taken up, and the assuaging of this guilt
and the expressing of unspoken love by painting flowers,
flowers, flowers; the physical distance between mother and
daughter and the mother's wishful thinking, on their first
day apart, that 'it won't seem very long' till the end of term;
the fact that in the 1950s a mother needed to write the first
letter while her daughter was still on the ship, so it would
be on the hall table at school on her arrival; the fact that a
mother with a small baby in Damascus in 1952 had time to
cover first pages of her letters with watercolours of flowers;
the brisk, cheerful, exclamation-marky prose not allowing
for any soppiness; the constant mention of the new baby
half-brother and his endearing (or maddening) ways; the
social life of the mother and stepfather (who was Minister
and then Ambassador), going off in their new Austen
Sheerline to visit 'the Fletchers'; the poignant mismatch of
the mother's interests and a schoolgirl's concerns.

'I had governesses from the age of 7 to 9,' Josceline told
me, 'and they were very unsatisfactory. One was an alco-
holic who got the DTs, and the next was mad, so she had to

go too. I wish I'd gone to the French School in Damascus. But my mother and stepfather decided to send me back to England. My baby half-brother was getting all my mother's attention.' Josceline remembers profound homesickness at first. 'I remember longing for my mother physically – just longing for her to bend towards me in her rustling evening dress and kiss me goodnight.'

People ask her, 'How on earth did you get through it?' The answer is simple. She had a kind and affectionate grandmother in London, Enid Jowett, wife of the painter P. H. Jowett and sister of Gilbert Ledward who sculpted the fountain in Sloane Square. Josceline's drawing-room in her house near Ravenscourt Park is full of paintings of and by these artistic grandparents. 'My grandmother gave *me* all her attention. She loved me unconditionally. That gave me complete security. My grandfather died when I was 10, so she needed me even more. We spent blissful school holidays together in London.'

At one time Josceline didn't see her mother for a year and a half. One day the headmistress of Knighton, Mrs Booker, said to her, 'Your mother's on the telephone. She's back in England. Come and see me when you've spoken to her.' Josceline picked up the receiver and said a tentative 'Hello?' 'I heard a voice saying "Hello, darling" – and I didn't recognize it.' The sensitive Mrs Booker had rightly guessed that she would be affected by this telephone call. 'I went to see her, and I was crying,' Josceline said.

*

This reminds us that it's the transitions that are painful. Being totally without one's parents can become oddly bearable, because you just have to forget about them and get on with life. It's the first hearing of the voice on the telephone after a long gap, or the anticipation of one's parents' arrival or their imminent departure, or a mother helping her daughter pack on the last afternoon of the holidays: these are the moments when sadness at separation can overcome us.

Brigid Waddams, on the last day of the holidays, used to cling to the banisters, hoping that if she clung hard enough she could avoid being sent back to the Franciscan convent in Taunton. It didn't work. The nuns told her that the reason her eyes were so pale was that she had cried all the colour out of them. 'I was utterly, utterly miserable,' Brigid said. 'We'd lived in India and up till then we'd been a tight family, facing the world abroad: a self-contained bundle of people. Kicked out of that bundle, I was desolate.'

Her parents had moved back to England and only lived thirty miles away, but it might as well have been on the other side of the world, because she hardly saw them. In the first week of term, before girls had settled, homesickness used to break out across dormitories: sobbing was contagious and soon the whole wing of a school could sound like a field of bleating lambs in search of their mothers.

Not seeing parents for a whole term was completely normal for boarding-school children in the 1930s, '40s and '50s; and not seeing them for a year or more was fairly common among children whose parents lived abroad. Girls and boys as young as 5 were subjected to the euphemistic 'entire charge'. The Truman & Knightley Directory advertisements say cheerful things like 'One holiday a year is spent away from Walmer, thus giving the children the necessary change of air and surroundings.' Children were escorted across London from terminal to terminal by unsmiling paid women from Universal Aunts. 'You didn't have to be bombed to have your life turned upside down,' Susie Vereker said to me – she was evacuated to South Africa and then sent to Cheltenham, and has written a moving book about her childhood of banishment, *The Yellow Duster Sisters*. 'Just the separation was traumatic enough: family relationships were never the same again.'

Anne Hancock, evacuated from Seadowns school near Rottingdean to Canada in 1941 and then sent to Cheltenham, didn't see her father (who was Chief Irrigation Officer in the Punjab) for eight years. Miss Martin, who ran Seadowns, 'thought imagination was bad for you and she took away my toys. I never knew what happened to them.' Anne arrived back in Liverpool from Canada at the end of the war and no one was there to meet her. Once, when she was older and at Cheltenham Ladies' College, her mother forgot which day term ended; Anne waited on the platform at Paddington and she didn't come.

'The schoolmistress said, "Where's your mother staying?" and I remembered it was in a hotel behind the Wallace Collection. So I had to go to that hotel, and the porter didn't know what to do with me. He put me in the Honeymoon Suite for the night.' That, Anne remembers, was a bewildering and lonely experience: the absolute opposite of a honeymoon. During the holidays she was sent to stay with 'Aunt Gladys and Uncle Tom' in Walton-on-Thames: not a real aunt or uncle, just distant friends of her parents whom she was expected to love as if they were a real aunt and uncle. 'There were dances and a tennis club, but I could never belong there. I did make one nice friend and we're still friends sixty years later.'

Daphne Rae, widow of the late headmaster of Westminster John Rae, was a girl with no parents at all. She was a ward of court from Ceylon, and had to make up her holidays as she went along. It was a childhood that taught her toughness and resourcefulness, and along the way she learned a great deal about the etiquette of being a guest in other people's houses.

Born in 1933, she was sent to board aged 4 in an establishment for both boys and girls near Altrincham: 'There were boys in my dorm,' Daphne said to me, sitting in the Army and Navy Club in St James's Square before taking the train back to Haslemere. 'It was a happy place, more like a home, and the under-matron used to sing Irish songs to us at night. One of the maids had a drip at the end of her nose and I hid behind a velvet curtain to see where the drop would fall.'

I liked those crystal-clear memories: the boys in the

dorm, the Irish songs, the drip on the nose. Those early years have been distilled down to those images in Daphne's mind. At 7 she was sent to Annisgarth School in Windermere, wearing the wrong clothes: 'they' (whoever 'they' were; even she wasn't sure, being a ward of court) had procured not quite the right uniform.

At the beginning of each holidays she was given a few tissue-paper-thin five-pound notes to pay for travel, and she relied totally on invitations from families to get her through till the next term. She made it her business never to be sent to stay in a 'holiday home' for wards of court and other waifs and strays. 'I was never short of an invitation. Right up to the end, though, I made a rule never to stay with anyone for more than two weeks. When I arrived at some-one's house they usually did something special: a cricket match, or a play, and I was always included.'

The most difficult dilemmas when she arrived at a new house were: did you make the bed yourself, and did the counterpane go over the eiderdown or was it the other way round? Did you eat your salad on the side plate or the main plate? 'All families were different. The first meal was a trial: I was always served first, being the visitor.' The first item she asked for on arrival at any house was a sheet of paper to write a thank-you letter to her hostess at the house she had just left. Thus she drifted around, through her whole childhood, gathering lifelong friends, and receiving her first-ever birthday present at the age of 14, near Inverness.

One day she was sent to a new school in Scotland, one

whose name she didn't know, arriving in the dark in the days before schools had their names on the gate. 'I was in a long dorm, and one of the girls had lost her Mason Pearson hairbrush. Where was it? The headmistress pointed at *me*. "Come with me," she said, and I followed her. She had a bun at the back of her head. I noticed the front door was ajar and I nipped out and ran away. I hitch-hiked to a house I'd been to stay at in the holidays, in the Borders.'

At their wits' end, her guardians eventually escorted her to Manchester station with a label round her neck saying 'Perth, Scotland'. 'They marched me down the platform and I was locked inside the guard's van. As soon as the train left, the kind guard moved me to a super carriage and I was given lovely food in the restaurant car. We arrived at Perth Station in a thunderstorm and I thought, "I'd better be the last person to get out, so the person who's waiting for me will know it's me." When I got out a lovely, small woman was standing there. "Where are your Wellingtons?" she asked. I had no suitable clothes and no suitcase; I was wearing the same underwear as I'd worn running away. We drove off into the night.'

This woman turned out to be Miss Ross, the much-loved headmistress of Craigmount School, evacuated to Scone Palace, a magical place where no one was wrongly accused of stealing hairbrushes. 'Everyone wore kilts,' said Daphne. 'I borrowed other people's, so I was a Fraser one week, a Campbell the next, a MacDonald the next ... If you're always arriving late and in the wrong clothes, you get used to fitting in. It was lovely. I knew every bit of the roof of Scone.'

The best friend Daphne made through all these years was a girl called Jane, the youngest of a family of nine siblings, and it was to her house that she went to stay most often – but still never for more than two weeks. It was not till the girls' mid-teens that Jane's father said to Daphne, 'I wish you could have stayed with us for longer. When you leave, Jane always gets another bout of asthma.'

It was almost as bad to be at boarding-school very near home: so near yet so far. Sheila Fowler-Watt, in the junior house at Roedean aged 8 in the late 1940s, could see her own house high up on the next hill. 'I don't think there was much difference from being on the other side of the world,' she said, 'as I was a full boarder. I was desperately homesick and tried to find places where I could hide to cry without being seen: cupboards, for instance. I found it very difficult when I heard somebody singing a song my nanny used to sing. That brought on a wave of homesickness.' Homesickness, like grief, comes in waves. In adult life Sheila went on to run a boarding-school, Brambletye in West Sussex, with her husband, 'and the first thing I did was to make sure new boys talked to me about their homesickness. I encouraged them to talk about it, and they laughed about my hiding in a cupboard.'

Victoria Mather was so homesick during her first term at Woldingham in Surrey in 1963 that she ran away after four weeks. 'I packed my "free-study case"', she told me, and walked down the drive to the station, which happened to be inside the school grounds. I waited till a train came. I was running away to my godfather who lived at the Savoy Hotel. He gave me the most delicious lunch – roast chicken. That made a change from the revolting food at Woldingham. I was taken back to the school and they were quite cross, and isolated me in the infirmary. They asked my mother to collect me, but she said she was far too ill – and I was still at the school six years later.' It was a school she came to love.

Often it was the pets, not the parents, that children most dreaded saying goodbye to. I met a contingent of West Heath Old Girls, all still close friends, who had been there together in the early 1950s, and they mentioned weeping but said firmly, 'It wasn't the parents.' 'On the last day of the holidays one would spend the whole day with one's ponies,' said Phoebe Berens, whose family lived in Scotland, 'kissing them, crying: up close with the pets.' I've read lots of letters to parents from boarding-school girls and many of them begin, "Dear Mummy and Daddy, How are the animals?"'

Brigid Keenan used to say to her sister, who was also at the Franciscan convent in Taunton, '*Please* cry. If we both cry, they'll take us away from here.' But her sister was happy and had no intention of crying. Girls from the same family could take things quite differently, and sometimes the girls you would expect to be robust were in tears, and the girls you would expect to be tearful were fine. The 8-year-old Catherine Freeman, on the train to the evacuated

Assumption Convent in Herefordshire in September 1939, wiped her tears away with the ears of her toy rabbit, 'and settled straight down to a richly interesting school life'.

How did the threads of family life hold together during the long months apart? Mother and daughter wrote to each other once a week: mothers (and, if you were lucky, fathers too) writing voluntarily, daughters because they had to write a letter home after church on Sunday, and letters were generally censored. When Ann Leslie tried to slip into her letter home that she was unhappy at the Presentation Convent at Matlock, the nun (censor with censer) said to her, 'You're being selfish, you know, as your parents are very far away and this would only upset them.'

It was no good trying to write home about some terrible injustice that had been done to you because, first, it would be censored, and second, even if it did get out and reach home, parents were not interested in getting involved in school disputes. They had handed their daughter over, to sink or swim and to learn life's lessons in the process. 'I was falsely accused,' remembers Vanessa Kent, who was at Roedean in the early 1960s. 'I tried to tell my mother about it but she just said, "That's life, darling, and you'd better just put up with it."'

So letters home had to be bland, overly upbeat affairs, often only just reaching the top of page two, and taken up with gushing descriptions of last night's fire practice. By far the most commonly used adjective in daughters' letters home was 'super'. Last night's fire practice was super, yesterday afternoon's walk was super, Gilly's birthday was super-*duper*: girls, sensitive to their parents' wishes, knew it was their duty to reassure them they were having a lovely time, even if they weren't.

The only plaintive note was in urgent pleas for replacement items that a girl had lost, or for vital bits of uniform she was missing: 'Please send me a new napkin ring' or 'We need *three* white blouses. Please could you order one from Daniel Neal's?' There were anxious requests from a powerless daughter to a mother who might have some clout with the headmistress: 'I think we're allowed an extra Sunday out next term so please can you write to Miss Salter ... '

At break-time the names of girls who had received letters from home were read out, or letters were put on the hall table. I remember a girl at Sibton Park who never had a letter from home, except once, but it was only a postcard and it didn't start with 'Dear', just with her name. The Matron read it out, as the handwriting was illegible, and it sounded chillingly loveless. Most parents did come up with the goods, but the content of their letters was often oddly disappointing. Mothers would prattle on about subjects of little interest to their daughters. There was a great deal about how the raspberry canes were coming on. 'My mother used to tell me how many brace of pheasant she'd shot, or how the garden was,' said Pat Doyne-Ditmas. "There was nothing asking me how *I* was, or who my teachers were. Really, I was packed off to Cheltenham and got rid of.'

'My parents,' said Anna Dalrymple, who was at Hanford School in the early 1970s, 'wrote me endless letters about what fun Goodwood or the Cheltenham Races were. They were very keen on hunting, racing, fishing, shooting, skiing and Paris.' Anna received hundreds of letters regaling her with news of the fun they were having.

There was a mystique about parcels. Letters only had words in them but parcels had a present. Or at least a napkin ring. Whatever it was, it was a thrill. Virginia Coates's grandmother used to send her pot-pourri and rose and violet creams, but what she longed for most was a boy's rugger shirt. Usually, any sweets or unsuitable books were confiscated unless the mother managed to conceal them cleverly inside something else.

Telephone calls were rare and upsetting. They only came into fashion in the late 1960s, when girls adopted the expression 'Please can I reverse the charges?' spoken to the operator. You had to queue for ages for the school's only telephone, listening in on other girls' conversations as you gradually came closer to hearing your own mother's voice, by which time you were feeling dizzy with homesickness. What if, after that long wait, no one answered the telephone because no one was at home? Girls sometimes cried all night after that trauma.

Even more taxing were the visits of parents to the school. In the 1940s this happened once a year or never; in the 1950s it was once a term, if the parents lived in the same country; and from then on it became more frequent but could still be embarrassing. The girls whose mothers came in mud-spattered Land Rovers wearing dowdy skirts and gumboots longed to have glamorous mothers who wore silk dresses and high heels; and vice versa. 'My mother was an ambassador's wife,' said Josceline Dimbleby, 'so she was too glamorous: I wrote a letter to her, pleading, "Please don't wear pink!"'

Cicely Taylor remembers a girl at Greycotes (the lovely prep-school she went to on the outskirts of Oxford) whose mother was much too close for comfort. The girl's name was Flavia and her mother pronounced it 'Flah-via'. Her mother was known as 'Miss Timpson': her daughters were supposedly adopted, though actually they were her own but she had never married. 'She rented a house opposite our boarding-house on the Marston Ferry Road, and every night she would wave goodnight to Flah-via,' said Cicely. 'In the mornings she would come in, take the sheets off her bed, air them and brush her hair. The school put up with that. Then Flavia went to Westonbirt and her mother took a room at the Hare and Hounds pub at the end of the drive. The poor girl almost had a nervous breakdown.'

The whole point of boarding-schools was that parents were not supposed to hover. At their best – and Greycotes, as we shall see in the next chapter, was an example of the best – these institutions gave girls a chance to form their own friendships without parental supervision.

As my parents lived half an hour's drive away I could

go home after church every other Sunday; and the words at the end of the Matins service, 'The peace of God which passeth all understanding keep your hearts and minds in the knowledge and love of God', are forever associated with the blissful knowledge that my parents were outside in the churchyard, waiting to scoop me up for the day. Going home created the parallel torment at the other end of the day of having to leave again – the terrible tea-time lurch in the stomach, the echoing plummet of which I still feel every Sunday evening forty years later.

For the large numbers of girls whose parents lived far away, the rare parental visits were spent having lunch or staying at a local hotel. Instead of chatting easily to their parents as they had in their pre-boarding childhoods, they found they were now having to make polite conversation with them in the hush of a hotel dining-room, often with other clusters of school families in the same room, all eavesdropping on each other. Topics ran dry; new opening gambits were tried; common ground was searched for; fathers looked at their watches: it was all a strain, and the lunch was expensive, and then they had the whole afternoon to get through until it was time to go back.

'My parents called them "the West Country exeats",' said Virginia Coates. 'I was at St Mary's, Shaftesbury and my brother was at Downside. My father had a special tweed suit for these exeats. We had to stay at the Royal Chase Hotel in Shaftesbury.' Judith Keppel remembers sitting around for hours with her parents at the Chequers Hotel in Newbury, trying to think of things to talk about. Sunday afternoons with the parents, not at home, could seem interminable.

One Old Girl I spoke to vividly remembers wishing her parents *would* take her and her sisters out to lunch in a cosy hotel, rather than shivering on a rug with a picnic in a rain-drenched field. There were two parent-related areas of anxiety for this girl and her sisters, who were at St Mary's, Ascot in the mid-1960s: first, their father was Anglican rather than Catholic and he didn't take the nuns quite seriously enough. On going-out days he would indulge his daughters in unsuitable pursuits such as beagling: their smart school uniforms would get covered with mud. 'He took us to the Guards' Boating Club in Maidenhead and hosed us down. We arrived back at school in a dreadful state. Those nuns did not understand mud.'

The second area of anxiety was that the girls' mother, never having been to school herself (she had been educated by a governess), had no conception of institutional rules and their importance to schoolgirls. 'We had to be back at St Mary's by 6 o'clock. You were almost murdered if you were late for Benediction. One day we were at the Fourth of June at Eton, where my brother was at school. At 4 o'clock I was already looking at my watch, beginning to fret about getting back on time. At 4.30 I saw the boot of our car go up and out came all my parents' bottles: gin, whisky, wine and cocktail glasses, and all their friends in hats started clustering round the car and a great big drinks party got going. "*Mum*," I tried to say, "I have to be back at school by 6." But she wasn't listening. It didn't mean anything to her. She was far too excited about being with her friends whom she didn't see enough of. There was a gulf of understanding between us.'

Six o'clock came and went, and so did seven and eight o'clock. 'My mother eventually got me back to school at nine. Everyone had been in bed for half an hour. To make it up to me, she gave me a smelly Pont l'Évêque cheese left over from the cocktail party. She thought that would cheer me up. She had no idea that what I needed most of all was to *conform*. What on earth was I supposed to do with that Pont l'Évêque? I hid it in the bracken and we feasted on it for the whole week, on the way back from hockey.'

The housemistress was extremely nice and gracious to her parents when they brought her back late. The next day, with the parents safely out of the way, Mother Bridget erupted in fury.

5

Some Rural Idylls

The essential characteristic of a headmistress, from a pupil's point of view – and it was a characteristic few parents checked up on when choosing a school for their daughter – was that the headmistress herself remembered what it had been like to be a young girl herself. I mentioned in the chapter on the Misses that some of them were kind: but it was more specifically the quality of empathy that some had and some lacked. An empathetic headmistress could create a world of happiness and kindness, even in a hideous building. An unempathetic one (or, worse, a pair of them) could create a world of misery and mistrust, even in a stately pile with the finest collection of rhododendrons in the country.

Some were so terrified of their authority being

undermined that they would never let on that they, too, had once been children. They had probably forgotten it themselves. Others had more confidence and a twinkle in their eye. Writing about the governance of Miss Dove, the founding headmistress of Wycombe Abbey, Lorna Flint coined a memorable phrase to describe a good leader: 'the heroism of the relaxed grip'.

The scene of girls in summer dresses rushing out into the garden after tea – which you can't help picturing when you imagine life at an idyllic girls' boarding-school – really did happen: there were blissful schools, tucked away in the country, where girls climbed trees and built dens with their friends for hours on end as daylight turned to dusk on June evenings, and where no one was being vile to anyone. We'll address the question of whether anyone was actually doing any work at such places in a later chapter. If you look at old photographs of such schools, the girls are smiling genuine giggly smiles of joy. Alexandra Etherington showed me photographs of her and her friends in kilts and blouses at Butterstone, near Dunkeld, in 1969, and I don't think I've ever seen such happy children. 'I can still name every girl in those photos,' said Alexandra. 'There were only forty of us, and you could take your pony.'

The last day of the holidays, for these girls, was spent not burying their tear-stained faces in their ponies' manes but preparing them for a journey. 'My mother would take me, my trunk and my baby brother in the car to Hanford,' said Anna Dalrymple, 'and, hitched to the back, was the trailer with my pony, Taffy.' On arrival at Hanford the pony was unpacked before the trunk.

This book is not about the present day, but I did visit Hanford School in 2014 and it is so unchanged from the way it was in 1947 when it was founded that to describe it now is to describe it then. The elegant, musty drawing-room is untouched and even smells like 1947: wood smoke and first editions of Stephen Spender. I arrived just as the eighty-five girls (aged from 8 to 13) were finishing their apricot crumble in the Jacobean dining-room with a min-strels' gallery. After lunch they rushed out into the grounds, some on to a makeshift hockey pitch, some to the health-giving outdoor pool, and some to the stables. I asked them whether they might be having any lessons later in the day. They weren't sure but thought probably not. A notice on the noticeboard said, 'Third Form new riders to sit on ponies so that we can see what ponies will suit.'

This is just how Hanford has always been. 'In the summer term,' said Anna Dalrymple, 'if you were in the top rides, you were woken early in the morning to ride up on to the twin hills near the school, Ham and Hod.' The top rides! I didn't even know that 'rides' were graded at girls' schools, or that there was a job called 'galloping matron'. At a gathering of Hanford Old Girls, held at Gigi Richardson's house, I met Lucinda Mowbray who had been a galloping matron at Hanford in the late 1970s, and I asked her what the job entailed. 'Get up, do your horse, get the girls up, fetch the ponies in, fold socks, sort clothes, have lunch with the children and take them for a ride,' she explained. Riding up on to those high hills at dawn was a treat that has sustained Hanford girls for years and given them a feeling of optimism.

One dormitory, Seymer, had such an ornate, high-relief fireplace that you could walk round the whole room, and up and over the fireplace, without touching the floor. 'You could climb up on to the lead roof of the house and run all the way round, like a rat track, ducking down when you passed the headmistress's office,' Anna said. The current girls' only gripe was that teddy bears were not allowed on fire-practices.

But there was fear, too: fear which Anna still describes as 'terror'. This was when the 'relaxed grip' suddenly tightened and girls found themselves in deep trouble. Anna lost every single item of clothing, one by one. Each was found and confiscated by the under-matrons, until at last she was made to wear nothing but her pyjamas and painting overall for a whole day. 'I had to walk the walk of shame, wearing the pyjamas and overall, along the minstrels' gallery during lunch, with the whole school looking up at me.'

If you were caught persistently talking after lights-out you were banished to sit either in the minstrels' gallery in the dark or, worse, in the dining-room with all the oranges on Bakelite plates laid out for the next morning's breakfast. The glowing oranges somehow looked scary in the middle of the night, Anna remembers, and once she saw a ghost, a grey lady gliding past making a 'crinoliney noise' as she passed.

Fern, the school's white Alsatian, wore a muzzle during the day but the muzzle was taken off at night. It was terrifying when Fern padded past you in the darkness.

Every rural idyll had its dark cloud. Before going to Beaufront, Georgina Hammick went to a wonderful prep-school called Cane End in Berkshire in 1946. The only dark cloud she can remember was a Scottish matron saying to her (after she had confessed to wetting the bed, aged 7), 'You're a duhrrty, duhrrty little girl.' But apart from that it was bliss. Hearing her talk about Cane End made it all the more painful to hear about the later move to Beaufront: a child's change of fortune for the worse is always hard to hear about. On first mentioning the Christmas term at Cane End she started to sing:

> *My counterpane is soft as silk,*
> *My blanket white as creamy milk,*
> *The hay was soft to Him, I know,*
> *Our little Lord of long ago.*

The gentle sweetness of that carol seemed to sum up the atmosphere of Cane End. 'They loved children,' Georgina said – 'they' being the staff (for example, Miss Tweedie in the art shed and Miss Harper for English) but chiefly the headmistress, Olive Howell, who looked like Virginia Woolf and who welcomed the children as if they were her family. There were boys as well as girls: they included Osbert

Lancaster's children Cara and William, John Piper's son Edward, and Alastair Sim's daughter Merlith.

'It was heavenly,' said Georgina. 'We were encouraged to do things we were good at. My sister and I were always asked to decorate the Christmas tree. It was so un-schooly: you could sleep in "the State Room". We were all living together in the whole of a country house. I remember the smell of freshly baked bread going along a passage: that was delicious.'

So, no lino-floor, behind-the-green-baize-door treatment for Cane End children. Organized afternoon walks were merry: there was a 'road walk' and a 'wood walk', and as they walked the children sang songs they knew by heart from the *Oxford Book of Folk Songs*. 'We were allowed to break out of the road walk and go across the fields and into the woods.' The heroism of the relaxed grip, indeed.

Some children were homesick and sobbed a great deal, but not Georgina and her sister, in spite of the fact that their father was military attaché in Washington DC and they didn't see their parents for a year. Their letters home were mostly drawings of ponies. They liked the riding mistress, Joan Fegan, who had 'a bright-white smile like Doris Day, wonderful teeth and a weather-beaten face, and she dressed like a chap. She was pretty no-nonsense: if you fell off she just said, "Don't be feeble," and you got on again.'

This reminds us that it is not soppy pampering that children need or even like. A bit of briskness from a weather-beaten riding mistress is welcome, teaching children to put

their misfortunes into perspective and not to wallow in
self-pity. What matters is that the briskness is powered by
genuine kindness.

In the winter of 1946–7, the Cane End children looked
after their own heifers, going out early in the morning to
break the ice in the troughs. This vignette leads us on to
our next rural idyll: the Farmhouse School at Wendover,
Buckinghamshire, to which Marigold Johnson was sent
during the war. It was started in the 1930s by 'a lame headmistress who had corgis', and who decided that hockey and
indeed all outdoor games were a waste of time and that girls
instead should learn animal husbandry.

'We had to put on jodhpurs and smocks and boots at 7
a.m.,' said Marigold, 'and go out and look after the animals: we graduated from rabbits and guinea-pigs to pigs,
then to goats, and then to cows. Once we spent a whole
night watching a sow give birth to ten piglets. And we
made butter.' During the days of the V2s in 1944 the girls
slept under rather than on their beds, with the counterpane
draped over the bed so it was like a tent. 'We loved it,' said
Marigold, 'but you couldn't sit up or your hair would get
tangled up in the bedsprings.'

Discipline was fairly lax. By the age of 10 or 11 girls were
secretly smoking, and their venue for this was the highly
inflammable hayloft. Lessons were taught by women from
outside the farm who had no idea what went on inside,
so the girls would suddenly say (in the middle of a Maths

lesson), 'We need to get the sheep in – it's raining,' and the teacher would let them go. Into this carefree agricultural environment came a glamorous pupil, the Princess of Siam. 'We adored her,' said Marigold. 'At the age of 11 she was already fully developed and fascinating: "Swami, tell us more!" we said, longing to hear more about her home life. She taught us how to be sophisticated.'

Greycotes, a prep-school on the northern edge of Oxford, was not exactly a *rural* idyll, but Cicely Taylor's description of life there was so countrified that I can't help putting it in this chapter. Again, the girls were trusted and given freedom. 'We all loved it,' said Cicely. 'The dorms were named after the Seven Dwarves. Sneezy was the sick-room; Sleepy was the babies, as young as 6. In summer we were allowed to take our beds out on to the veranda and sleep outside.'

Early on summer mornings the girls used to creep out of school and go down to the river for a swim on their own. The horsey girls used to get on to horses and ride them round the field, bareback. 'Once,' said Cicely, 'we stole some tins from the larder and we made a fire in a deserted old farmhouse. We cooked baked beans and had them for breakfast. We came back and our housemistress, lovely Miss Cornwall, noticed the smell of wood smoke in our hair, but she wasn't cross: she just told us to wash our hair so the headmistress wouldn't notice.'

Again, having in one's memory a day that began in that way has given the girls who took part a sense that any day *could* begin like that: that the world is a kind place and spontaneity is always possible. 'There was a girl in a wheelchair who'd had polio,' Cicely said, 'and she came everywhere with us – everyone pushed her around. Years later she started the Disabled Living Foundation.' Empathy breeds empathy.

Knighton House in Dorset, the prep-school to which Josceline Dimbleby went, was another kind place, as we have seen from the glimpse of Mrs Booker sensitively fore-seeing the effect on Josceline of a telephone call from her long-absent mother. 'The school was very good at music and artistic things,' Josceline said, 'and they didn't care too much about gym. The Bookers were a family and they made the children feel like a family. Girls were always going into Mrs B's study to chat with her. She was serene-looking, and her face looked as if it had soft down on it. She was quite godly, and at that age I was very happy to be godly.'

The matron was known as 'Nanny', and she had been the nanny to Mr and Mrs Booker's children. 'There was another nanny, another great comfort to me,' said Josceline. 'She used to sit me on her knee. The whole atmosphere of the place was kind. Boarding-schools like that were incredibly important for children whose parents lived abroad.'

Patricia Daunt, mother of James who founded Daunt Books, went at the age of 9 to a school called Langford Grove in Sussex, founded in the 1930s by Mrs Curtis, and full of her friends' children such as the Gathorne-Hardys and the Ponsonbys. (It's true: the schools in this happiest-chapter-so-far seem to have been run by women called 'Mrs' rather than 'Miss'.) What Mrs Curtis cared most about was that the ninety girls in her charge should be in a beautiful house, surrounded by lovely paintings and beautiful objects, and that they should hear wonderful classical music and thus develop their aesthetic tastes. This was exactly what happened. The English teacher Mrs Blythe gave Patricia a life-long love of reading, starting her on *Jane Eyre* at the age of 9. The music teachers, Mrs Kopp (an Austrian refugee) and Mr Boom, took out their instruments in the evenings and played: the girls drifted off to sleep to the distant sound of string quartets. Mrs Curtis took the girls to hear Thomas Beecham conducting in Brighton and to rehearsals at Glyndebourne.

'We were completely free,' said Patricia, 'so free that I got into the habit of running home, which was three miles away down the river, just so I could have a ride.' This all worked well, until one day Patricia was so late back to school that Mrs Curtis was in a panic and her parents were summoned, 'and I was told I was insufferable. Some neighbours of ours had a governess and they were looking for a third child, so I was sent off there – it was cheaper than Langford Grove. There I had the unhappiest two terms of my life. The two girls were beastly to me and I hated the governess.' That horrible phase ended when Patricia's father came to collect her and the family's bull-terrier bit him. 'That was *it*. Then I was sent straight to Southover.'

It is the change of fortune for the worse, again, that illuminates the joyousness of the nicer place. Another example of this is Gillian Darley's experience, first of the prep-school Riddlesworth Hall in Norfolk in the mid-1950s, and then of Benenden. Riddlesworth Hall happened to be run by someone called Miss Ridsdale, known as Riddy. 'What I remember most about Riddy was her *warmth*,' said Gillian. 'I remember her making me feel as if I counted for something.'

Before telling me in detail about Riddlesworth life, Gillian rhapsodized briefly about her red leather writing-case and her wicker sewing-basket. I think we've forgotten just how exciting such possessions were in the 1950s, '60s and '70s. Girls who had been given mere jigsaw puzzles for their birthdays, or at the most a packet of colouring pencils, felt elevated to a new maturity on being given a writing-case and sewing-basket of their very own on starting at boarding-school. These became a girl's treasured items. The leather-scented writing-case had pockets for envelopes and postcards and slots for pens, and it snapped open with a symmetrical twin-thumbed click. The sewing-basket had a covering of floral material over the lid and made a delicate wicker-creaking noise as you opened it. It contained reels of cotton of every colour, a packet of needles peaking at the longest, a pair of tiny gold-coloured scissors and, if you were lucky, a needle-threader.

It helped that the grounds of Riddlesworth Hall were 'completely lovely', Gillian said, with a shrubbery in which girls lived whole lives of the imagination among the bushes. 'There were hours and hours of people not asking where you were, and that was blissful.'

You were allowed to keep a small animal, for which you were solely responsible. Rabbits were the most popular: Gillian's was called Mr Bunter. Every evening the girls went into the grounds before bedtime to forage for their animals, and this searching for the choicest, most succulent grasses gave Gillian 'an intimate sense of the *place*'. One of the girls, who would now be classed as 'special needs', used to take her rabbit out and put it into other cages for the night. There was a sudden upsurge in the rabbit population. 'At any other school, I suppose,' said Gillian, 'she would have been lighting fires in the wastepaper-baskets.'

Riddlesworth was a beautiful 1911 house: Gillian was to become an architectural writer, and her love of architecture was born there. Even the dormitories had wonderful wallpapers to look at when you were ill. Miss Ridsdale cared about educating the girls' artistic tastes. They were read to every evening. 'Riddy's real *thing*,' Gillian said, 'was craft: sticking straw into wet clay to make model Saxon houses and so on. I've still got five things I made out of basketwork, including a wastepaper-basket and a lemonade tray. We did our crafts in a lovely cobbled courtyard, and they were a pleasure. That's exactly what they were meant to be: a delight and a pleasure.'

It was the contrasting attitude to hobbies at Benenden that summed up Gillian's dislike of that school, to which she went on in 1961. 'Benenden was a school based on excellence and competition. All those crafts I'd done for pleasure at Riddlesworth were now being *judged*. I made an album of photographs I'd taken of abbeys in Yorkshire, and it was judged not particularly good. I didn't *want* to win a competition. Then I made a green denim shirtwaister. It was judged to be so bad that it was called a "chuck-out" – not only did it win no points for my house, it actually subtracted from the house effort.'

The counties of Britain abounded with small private schools hidden away down long drives, and it was often a matter of luck whether a girl went to a kind one or a mean one, so little did most parents pay attention to the delicate matter of atmosphere. Also, perhaps, institutions are good at hiding the truth from visitors, so you only find out what a place is really like once you're properly installed, by which time it's too late.

'My parents didn't care a bit,' said Cecily Scott, who went to Merton Hall in Norfolk during the war. 'They were thankful if I had *any* education.' Merton Hall was run by Lord and Lady Walsingham, who had started the school in their house to educate their five children. 'All we did was ride,' said Carole-Anne Phillips, who was there at the same time as Cecily: 'ride and have fun. There were 60 girls. It was the most beautiful Elizabethan house, with linen-fold panelling and a long-room with two fireplaces. We roasted chestnuts on the huge log fires.'

'They [Lord and Lady Walsingham] were more interested in our learning about the horses than about academic subjects,' said Cecily. 'I was over the horsey phase by the age of 13 so I do wish the curriculum had been slightly more interesting. Really we were completely ignorant.'

But, as we'll see in the next chapter, even a fundamentally well-meaning school in an idyllic setting could be far from idyllic.

6

Hopelessness – and a School Called 'Wings'

With the best of intentions, a girls' country boarding-school could tip over from just about adequate to utterly, comically, tragically hopeless. A girl could find herself at such a place, stranded, miles from anywhere, with neither of her parents remotely interested in hearing any bad news. The daughter just had to go there, and go there again for another term, and another, as things got progressively worse.

When Jennifer McGrandle described Ryton Hall in Shropshire to me, to which she went from 1945 to 1949, she wanted to make it clear that there were a great many schools just like it: Ryton Hall was far from unique. This didn't make her feel better: it made her feel worse.

The flimsy prospectus should have given a warning sign to her parents, but it didn't. Some schools proudly stated that they were 'Recognized as efficient by the Ministry of Education'. Some were merely 'Recognized by the Ministry of Education'. Some weren't even recognized, and Ryton was one of these. In the four years that Jennifer was there, no one ever came to inspect the school or remembered anyone ever having inspected it. A private school could simply open its doors and exist, relying on the goodwill and the fees of parents happy to pay for their daughter to be in a pretty country house where she would mix with the right kind of children and learn good manners.

Here are some Ryton Hall prospectus quotes:

The entry of all examinations is purely optional, and every effort is made to give a wide education on modern lines combined with the advantages of home life.

It sounds a happy place; but 'of' is the wrong word there: parents should perhaps have been concerned about the imperfect English, let alone the optional nature of exams.

Beside organized Games there are other outdoor occupations: gardening, rambles, croquet, clock golf and tenniquoits. Picnics and excursions to places of interest, Exhibitions, etc, are planned.

I'm not quite sure about that capital 'E' for 'Exhibitions', but it sounds ambitious enough. Well, said Jennifer, the games field wasn't levelled and was ankle-deep in thistles.

They never played croquet, clock golf or tenniquoits. Instead they played half-hearted games of lacrosse, tennis and rounders. They never went to an Exhibition although they did once go for a lovely day-long ride with a picnic. There was a Nissen hut: that was the equivalent of the gym.

The escort meets the Scotch train at Crewe.

That sounds impressive: a whole escort going to meet 'the Scotch train'. Actually, said Jennifer, there was one girl who came from as far away as Wigan. There was no one from Scotland. The vast majority of girls were local.

The academic standard of Ryton Hall was 'diabolical', said Jennifer. 'I was two and a half years younger than the other girls in my class. And my parents never did anything about it. I don't think it particularly concerned them. My father had been posted to Shropshire, but was then posted to an air station in Dorset – and I was stranded in Shropshire for four years.'

Jennifer showed me the 1948 school photograph. The headmistress Miss Stirling – May Stirling; the girls called her 'Aunt May' – sits in the middle of her forty-seven per-fectly happy-looking girls, with a dog on her lap and her retinue of female members of staff next to her: the only man about the place was the boiler man. The forty-seven girls were aged between 5 and 16: that age-range was 'simply not viable', Jennifer said. May Stirling was 'a lovely woman, a JP with a strong Christian faith', but she couldn't attract good staff and couldn't even keep the second-rate staff she did manage to attract.

Another line from the prospectus:

There is a good library in the school to which new books are constantly being added.

Actually, said Jennifer, the 'library' consisted of two small shelves of books behind the closed doors of a cupboard. There was one good book, about Harrow, called *The Hill*, which she read and reread with fascination. But the under-nourishment of that minuscule library left her without a lifelong reading habit.

There was no science, and the French teaching was appall-ing. When Jennifer applied to Cheltenham Ladies' College the school secretary said, 'We're going to tell them you've only done French for two years', whereas she had actually done it for four. With no conception of the academic level of her pupils in the outside world, May Stirling entered Jennifer for a scholar-ship to Cheltenham, following which her mother was told by Cheltenham that her daughter was 'nowhere near scholarship standard'. 'That was purgatory for me,' said Jennifer, 'and cruelty.' She did get into Cheltenham, though; and there she was two years *older* than the youngest girl in her class.

The 9-year-old Caroline Cranbrook was taken to the International Horse Show by her parents in 1945. One of the schools taking part was a school called Wings.

'Caroline's so horsey, she might as well go and learn about horses,' said her father to her mother. 'Let's send her to Wings.' It was another example of a snap decision made by a father about schooling for his daughter.

'Why was it called "Wings"?' I asked Caroline when I went to visit her at her house in Suffolk. (There I made friends with her famous dog, Domino, who had recently vanished down a rabbit hole and had been missing for three whole weeks, presumed dead. Then, one morning, on the day of St Jude, the patron saint of lost causes, there was a violent storm that uprooted a tree, making a miracle possible: the family looked out of the window and saw Domino, thin but alive, limping her way home across the lawn.)

'Well,' Caroline said, 'It's a quote from Plato. "By beauty, truth and love the wings of the soul grow apace", or something. Wings had very high ideals. It was all about belief in the individual. To start with it was fine, but it gradually deteriorated and by the time I was there the staff were starting to leave. We were strictly instructed never, ever to "betray" the school by speaking badly of it to anyone outside.'

It almost goes without saying that Wings was in a beautiful Elizabethan house. So many schools were; and this was one of their big draws. Parents hoping their daughters would marry well wanted them to acquire an early taste for living in a house with multiple mullioned windows. Wings was in Charlton Park in Wiltshire: mullioned up to the eaves, with plentiful turrets.

The headmistress was out of her depth, and a heavy drinker. 'Every Saturday night we had ballroom dancing in the great marble hall,' said Caroline, 'and the headmistress sat drumming her fingers, with a cigarette hanging out of her mouth and a glass of crème de menthe. We had to dance with her father, who'd been wounded as a sapper in the First World War: either he had his "arms" on, with black gloves, or he couldn't be bothered to put them on and we just had to dance with the stumps.' Oddly enough, the school sport was rugby: the headmistress seemed to enjoy this. 'Jump on me, girls, jump on me!' she would say.

Biology was taught in the old kitchen. Supervised by the science mistress, the girls dissected an aborted foal, pegging it out on the kitchen table – 'and it stayed there for the whole term, pegged out like that, and soaked in formalin which made us all cry'.

When the teachers started to leave, one by one, the older girls were instructed to take over from them. Caroline, aged 15, was given the job of teaching biology and geography to the younger girls. Somehow the school had got on to a list of suitable schools for foreign girls, so Greek, French and Thai pupils started to arrive, hoping for a good British education. 'I tried to teach them about the reproduction of the amoeba,' said Caroline. 'I had a lump of cotton wool and I made a nucleus, and then I wetted it and tried to show them how it divided, and it wouldn't divide at all. I remember their utterly bewildered faces.'

As a prefect, not only did she have to teach the younger

children: she was expected to look after them as well. There were 5-year-olds, whose parents were in Africa: she had to look after them, bath them and put them to bed. One of her duties was to go out and retrieve children who were trying to run away down the mile-long drive.

The school was inspected while Caroline was there; she had make-up put on her face for the occasion, so she could pass for a teacher.

Eventually she could take it no more: she wrote a letter – '*the* letter' – to her parents, telling them exactly what was going on: it was an SOS and she managed to smuggle it out and post it, breaking the rules about not betraying the place. She still has the letter and she showed it to me as we sat by the fire in her study. In neat handwriting she explains to her parents that most of the staff are on the verge of collapse, suffering from exhaustion and overwork, and that they are about to leave. She describes her typical school day, getting up at 6.30 to do duties, including washing out the baths, putting the breakfast out, doing the washing-up, inspecting shoes and rooms, bathing, putting to bed and listening to the prayers of tiny children, and teaching. The school, she says, is on its last legs and the headmistress is on the verge of madness.

Her parents did take her away and sent her to the infinitely nicer Cranborne Chase.

Wings closed in the early 1950s. It was rumoured that the headmistress had knocked out a girl's tooth in assembly, when she didn't like the way she was looking at her.

7

Auras and Evacuations

Sometimes, all the various recurring themes I've been noticing while researching this book are horrifyingly concentrated into one moment for a particular girl: homesickness, discomfort, chilblains, feelings of alienation, long separation from parents, meanness of a pair of unmarried headmistresses, petty rules, uncomfortable uniform, boring Sundays, sense of bewilderment. I felt a strong simultaneous combustion of all these themes when Helen Holland described life at St Bride's, Helensburgh near Glasgow, to which she and her sister were sent at the age of 8 and 6 in 1953.

The school was run by Miss Auchterlonie and Miss Coventry. One was fat and one was thin. They were 'terribly severe': Miss Coventry poked the girls in their ribs with her stick if they weren't standing up straight while lining up to wash.

At one of the morning distributions of letters from home, Miss Auchterlonie read aloud a letter to a young girl who was not old enough to decode her mother's handwriting. 'Darling Patricia,' the letter went, 'we are all well and we hope you are too ...' and so on, and it ended 'Lots of love from Mummy.'

'That's ridiculous!' snapped Miss Auchterlonie. 'Who would love a wicked wee girl like you?'

That's enough: in a nutshell we have the whole aura of St Bride's. We can imagine Miss Auchterlonie ('rounded like a cottage loaf', if you want to know the details, 'with a very firm, tightly controlled, unmotherly bosom') and her side-kick Miss Coventry ('small and bent and scraggy'); we can imagine the girls being marched to church, two by two, in their regulation green Sunday coats, and being reprimanded if they forgot to wear their gloves, and having not enough to do on Sunday afternoons, and being discouraged from mixing with girls in different years – so Helen and her sister (both half-Jamaican and homesick and not seeing their parents for ten months) could not comfort each other – and no one ever being hugged or comforted.

Helen got eczema from the rage and her sister got asthma from the choking sobs. They both went on to have five children each: the antidote to childhood separation from family.

*

This is a chapter about auras: hearty, bookish, bleak, social, aesthetic or pious. You can tell something about the aura of a school from the names it gives its houses or its dormitories. Roedean's houses were (and still are) called House 1, House 2, House 3 and House 4, which somehow suit a gamesy school on a cliff above Brighton, whereas the houses at Queen Ethelberga's, Harrogate were more romantically called Darwent, Eofowick, Lyminge and Cantwara – all Kentish-Saxon names in honour of the Saxon Queen Ethelberga.

The houses at St James's, West Malvern were abstracts: Valiant, Discovery, Renown and Endeavour. We've already heard about the menacingly gung-ho names of the 'patrols' at Beaufront. The St Elphin's, Darley Dale houses were named after bishops: Selwyn, Gresford, Kennedy, Powys and Piggott. At the aforementioned Wings the houses were called (inevitably) Athene, Artemis and Aphrodite.

The dormitories at Moira House in Eastbourne were called Avalon, Galahad and Merlin; at West Heath they were named after flowers. In general, the more airy-fairy the names, the more relaxed the place but the worse the education. If I'd been a prospective parent I would have thought hard about these names before committing my daughter. As we have seen, though, few did.

Clothes lists also give a sense of a school's aura. Helen Holland sent me a copy of the St Bride's list and it is one of the iciest documents I've ever read. The nouns (as in school histories) have initial capital letters, emphasizing their importance and indispensability:

Woven Knickers to match Gym Tunic; 2 prs woollen
with 4 prs cotton linings for Winter; 3 prs cotton for
Summer.

2 School Cardigans (not Lumberjackets), green.

1 Green Dress for formal occasions (school pattern).

3 Green School Overalls (2 for House and 1 for School
use).

1 pr grey Worsted Shorts (school pattern only) . . .

and so on, going on for two and a half pages and ending
with the command that everything must be 'distinctly
marked with Christian name and Surname in Cash's woven
name tapes', and that 'clothing and personal belongings
extra to this list and jewellery (except brooch, watch and one
simple necklace) should not be brought to school'. There's
no mention of any comforting item such as 'soft toy' or
'photograph frame'. Travelling across land and sea, dragging
enormous school trunks, St Bride's girls had to bring eight
different pairs of shoes ranging from Bedroom Slippers to
Wellington Boots.

Schools tended to keep their aura even when they were
evacuated. When Barbara Kenyon was at Roedean in June
1940 she wrote to her mother, 'It's terribly exciting, we can
hear the guns on the French coast!' This was not the ideal
place for schoolgirls to be, and the school moved to the
Station Hotel in Keswick, where it stayed until 1944. There,
all the heartiness of Roedean life continued: the girls played

lacrosse on the town field, against each other as there was no one else to play against. Benenden girls, meanwhile, evacuated to the Hotel Bristol in Newquay, were playing lacrosse against each other at low tide on the Newquay beach.

The Keswick Station Hotel wasn't big enough for all school activities, so some lessons were taught in the station waiting-room. Passengers wandering in to ask about the time of the next train to Penrith found a form of uniformed girls in the middle of a geography lesson on how to find the source of the River Nile. One of the attractions of Roedcan was that it was ahead of its time in terms of science teaching: the hotel conservatory was converted into a lab. Art was taught in the hotel garage. I asked Barbara what her most vivid memory of Keswick was and she said, 'the rain'.

Katharine Whitehorn was also evacuated to Keswick, and for her it was 'hell'. 'I hated games and didn't have any friends,' she told me in her kitchen in Hampstead. 'New Girls were treated as absolute scum for the first half of term.' Coming from a nonconformist, left-wing-leaning, non-commercially-minded family, Katharine felt totally out of place in the Roedean aura, and she liked the moment when her visiting father patted the bottom of the full-size statue of a black woman (which happened to stand in the hall of the Keswick Station Hotel) and said to the headmistress, 'Distinguished Old Girl, no doubt?' There were, in fact, no 'Old Girls of colour' in those days.

After two years, Katharine ran away – actually, cycled

away – to St Bee's School, on the coast, where her father was a teacher at the evacuated Mill Hill School. 'What happened after that was lovely. My father said there was no point in forcing me to go back to Keswick, as "it would ill befit me to be seen fighting with my daughter on St Bee's platform". My mother arranged for me to go to Glasgow High School and lodge with a local family. There, instead of being treated as scum in my first term, I was invited to tea with a family two days after arriving. Ever since that moment, I've known I'm happy when I'm happy.'

Tudor Hall was evacuated to Burnt Norton in the Cotswolds in 1939 and its friendly, arts-loving aura came with it – and came with it again when it moved to its later location in Oxfordshire. I've always found the name 'Tudor Hall' rather suspicious: I mean, no one called their grand houses 'Elizabethan Hall' or 'Jacobean Manor'. It turns out that Tudor Hall was the name not of a stately home but of the mock-Tudor mansion in Forest Hill, south London, where the school was from 1850 to 1908.

Nesta Inglis, its much-loved headmistress from 1935 to 1965, was another example of an unmarried woman who devoted her life to running a boarding-school; her niece Jane Goddard told me that Nesta's adored older brother had been killed in the First World War and that no man had ever come up to his standard. Nesta herself had been educated at Tudor Hall when it was at another suburban house called Southlands in Chislehurst, after Forest Hill.

No great intellectual, with no university education, and not particularly well-read, she nonetheless managed to come up with a Latin school motto which included a subjunctive: *Habeo ut dem*. Because the girls 'had', they were inspired and trained to 'give'.

Nesta herself certainly gave. During the school holidays of 1940, '41 and '42 she invited London parents and siblings to come and stay at Burnt Norton with the girls to escape from the Blitz. Jane Goddard remembers this as 'absolute bliss'; and, after thinking about the long separations of girls from their parents, we can imagine the joy of having your parents and brothers and sisters to stay with you at school for a wartime Christmas in beautiful safe Burnt Norton with its magical gardens, where the fathers joined in vigorous games of hide-and-seek. 'Did you all have stockings on Christmas morning?' I asked Jane, to which she gave me an emphatic 'yes'.

After the war, in typical fearless-unmarried-headmistress fashion, Nesta Inglis picked up a stately home, Wickham Park, 'for a song' (£15,000), and the school moved there, where it remains to this day. 'Its reputation under Nesta was not particularly for academics,' said Jane Goddard. 'It was for turning out nice girls. Nesta wanted us to be good to each other, polite and above all kind. She never talked to us as "girls", only "children": I liked that. "Girls" sounded rather military.' Many of the pupils at Tudor Hall were 'madly horsey': it was full of girls from Oxfordshire and Gloucestershire hunting families. They also did a great deal of folk-dancing because Nesta loved it. There were folk-dance displays on the lawn in the summer term, with the music mistress thumping out the piano accompaniment. Thus the aura deepened: kindness, horsiness, dancing, good taste, good works.

Sometimes evacuation could be too much of a good thing. Penrhos College never really got over the glory of being evacuated to Chatsworth. When Morag Bushell was there in the 1970s the staff were still going on about the great days at Chatsworth and the school was still being run on a war footing, with jam every other day and honey once a week. The antiquated German textbooks, still in Gothic script, were all about a 1930s German family who kept a dachshund and gave 'Heil Hitler' salutes. No post-war excitement could live up to the thrill of evacuation upgrade (as rapturously described in *Penrhos: The Second Fifty Years*):

> Miss Edman set off, accompanied by Miss F. M. Dodd, to contact the Devonshire family, and with them prepare for their departure and Penrhos's arrival. It was a daunting undertaking, for it was hard to visualize Staff bedrooms and dormitories, form rooms and dining halls in the vast and lovely ducal rooms, and to add to the confusion the Chatsworth Staff were clearing up after the festivities held for the coming-of-age of the Duke's heir, the Marquis of Hartington.

The evacuated girls draped the chilly naked Chatsworth statues (such as *Mercury* in the Painted Hall) with school scarves and the occasional bra, or 'bb' as bras were then called. That was the limit of naughtiness in those compliant days. 'Physics', the history tells us, 'was held in the butler's pantry, Biology in the stillroom, and Chemistry, in the interest of safety, in the stables.' In 1957, back home in Colwyn Bay, the school erected a new three-storey building for Physics and Domestic Science. The new building was officially named 'Chatsworth'.

St Felix, Southwold was evacuated to Tintagel: Erica Burgon describes a classroom on the path halfway down to the beach, and she remembers the gym staff sitting on the beach all morning waiting for different groups of girls to come down for their gym sessions. After Tintagel, the school moved to Hinton House in Somerset, where there were no replacement bulbs for the candelabra, so it became harder and harder to read the words of the assembly hymns as the war went on.

Tanya Harrod was at St Felix in the mid-1960s; she described a place of order and beauty, 'like a magic kingdom'. 'For years afterwards I used to dream about it,' she said; 'I was living my adult life and I was suddenly back there in that beautiful closed world.' The spirit of the school seemed to stay with St Felix wherever it was. The house names included Fawcett (after Millicent Fawcett, non-militant suffragist), Brontë and Somerville: names to inspire girls.

Tanya's recollections remind us that order does not have to be terrifying or punishing. At its best an enclosed, ordered world could give girls a sense of security in which to blossom and flourish. At the more brutal schools, the constant ringing of bells made them feel they were perpetually late for something. At a kinder school such as St Felix, the gentle dinging of the bell divided the day benignly into its different ceremonies.

'At first,' said Tanya, 'it seemed like a nightmare not to have one's privacy. We weren't allowed to read after lights-out and I remember our housemistress confiscating our light bulbs. That happened when I was sharing a room with a girl called Retina Lonbay – her father was a doctor and had taken a stab at the medical dictionary to find a name for her.' But the beauty of the physical environment worked its magic: 'red brick with white paintwork, sweetness and light, a beautiful library with good paintings, an altarpiece in the chapel, School of Filippino Lippi, and Stanley Spencer had done a wonderful drawing of one of the early headmistresses. There was always a lovely smell of polish, and flower arrangements on the table outside the headmistress's study, and in the hall of each house.'

Such touches make the difference. Some schools, and St Felix was one of them, aimed to shape the girls' aesthetic tastes and teach them to love beauty and the arts. Cloistered there, Tanya and her friends read their way through the library – 'We started with Oscar Wilde; we worshipped him;

and we went on to Rupert Brooke and Auden.' They were taken to see Benjamin Britten conducting at Snape. Tanya appreciated the 'ceremonial qualities of the life': on Sunday evenings, dressed in their green Sunday dresses, known as 'green slimes', the girls clustered round their housemistress, the sprightly Miss Turner, in her drawing-room. 'We'd just make conversation. That was the point of it.'

In the dining-room, also, the girls took turns at High Table, where they were expected to make conversation with visiting Old Girls, 'who often seemed to be missionaries, with carousels of slides telling us about their travels'. (I've been collecting 'Titles of Sunday-evening lectures by visiting Old Girls' while researching this book. 'Eagles: Monarchs of the Air' is a typical one; and, pre-1953, 'The Latest Attempt on Everest'. The lecture I'm glad I didn't have to sit through was one at Cheltenham in 1952, 'The Great King and His Palaces', 'illustrated by the epidiascope, and enlivened by Miss Grant's anecdotes of her travels in Iran'. 'Enlivened' is surely a euphemism for 'made longer'.)

Once you surrender to such an ordered daily life, you can even start finding the uniform romantic. Tanya Harrod did. 'In the spring term at St Felix we had to make our own gathered gingham summer skirts. I remember the business of putting on the waistband. We laughed about it then, but there was a real romance about the uniform: the dark-green gymslip, the blouse with a rounded collar, the gold-coloured jersey, the green over-pants to wear over underpants, and the stockings we mended ourselves. And the dark-green cloaks with hoods lined in our house colours.' There was a rule about not speaking or running in the corridors, 'but that didn't make life dull. We did so much laughing: there was a high level of emotional attachment.'

Every outing was an adventure. 'The wonderful history teacher Miss Leiching took us to Ipswich Poly for lectures,' Tanya said. 'We'd stop at the motorway café on the way back for a bacon sandwich: that was crazily exciting. Every summer there was a house picnic: the whole house went off in a bus. Once we went to Beccles where we rowed upstream, made a fire and cooked our picnic on a stove. There was a moment in the summer term when we were allowed bare legs and shirtsleeves – no more socks or stockings. When we were in our last year we were allowed bikes, and we cycled to the fudge shop in Southwold: I remember the balminess and the scent of gorse.' The judicious, not-too-liberal awarding of treats and privileges made each one unforgettably delicious.

Cranborne Chase in Dorset (always known as Crichel because it was in a stately home called Crichel House) also had this aesthetic aura. Founded after the war as a sort of Bryanston for girls, 'it lacked real academic go-ahead,' said Josceline Dimbleby, who went there in 1956, 'but it fed your mind and your imagination and your *taste*. We were terribly disapproving of things we didn't like – for example, tiered skirts.'

She showed me photographs of her friends posing pensively in front of Grecian urns and gravestones: their vision of beauty. There were joint productions of Gilbert and Sullivan operas with the boys at Bryanston; one of Josceline's friends was madly in love with John Eliot Gardiner, and she literally wilted as a fairy in *Iolanthe* when on stage with him. The girls were steeped in music, and Josceline went on to the Conservatoire in Lausanne and then to the Guildhall to study singing.

The auras of Southover, Heathfield and West Heath were more social, although these schools did also nurture girls' artistic tastes. Southover was known as 'the school where everyone married everyone else's brothers'; and those brothers would certainly have been members of the landed gentry or above. If you read the list of pupils' addresses at the back of the Southover school magazines of those days you find a mouthwatering selection of old rectories, castles, manor houses and farms. The acceptable home address was: name of large house; village it was quite near; county. It was not done to live at any kind of obscure urban address, such as 24 Whitfield Road, Haslemere. Only about one girl in the whole list did live at that kind of address and I pity her, because it stands out. If you did have an urban address it had to be a London one, and ideally Cadogan, Belgrave or Eaton something.

As we'll see in the final chapter, lifelong friendships are one of the finest fruits of a boarding existence, and friendships

forged at these schools seem particularly strong and definitely 'out of the same hat-box'. While I chatted for half
an hour to Laura Lonsdale, who was at West Heath in the
1970s (at the same time as Diana, Princess of Wales), she
received at least ten text messages from different friends,
many of them ex-school friends. 'I'm a people person,' she
admitted; and those schools were ideal for people people.
If you chat to a 1970s Heathfield Old Girl it won't be long
before she asks you whether you know Poppy Delevingne,
Tiggy Legge-Bourke and Gilly Ogilvy-Wedderburn. These
schools were chosen by parents who wanted their girls to be
part of the right set, for life.

Deportment at these schools was part of the curriculum:
it was said that you could spot a Heathfield girl anywhere
in the world by the way she got in and out of a car. At St
James's, West Malvern (almost as high on the social ladder
as Heathfield), there was an annual deportment competition; as Fiona Buchanan remembers, it was run as a series
of elimination rounds. 'The Deportment Prize was the only
prize I ever won. All the girls had to walk round and round
the only level part of the grounds, and girls were plucked
out if their deportment was flawed in any way. The last girl
walking won the prize.' The great St James's tome, *I Was
There*, has a vignette of a 1930s deportment teacher at work,
preparing the girls for life's social emergencies:

You are alone in your mother's drawing-room. The door
opens and the maid announces a caller. What will you

do? Not, I hope, blush and run away, muttering something about fetching your mother. The maid will do that. No, you must rise gracefully, resting your weight on your back foot as you do so; you must come forward, put out your hand with an agreeable smile, and say . . .

And there the example tantalizingly ends.

Heathfield had an edge of piety about it, being 'sensationally High Church', as the group of 1970s Old Girls I met recalled. 'We had to wear a chapel cap, made of nets, pleated and tied at the back, and we used to process down the passage and down the aisle of the chapel, morning and evening.' By the 1970s this piety was beginning to descend into helpless giggles: 'The chaplain, Mr Stride, decided to do a re-enactment of the Last Supper. He was Jesus, and we were his disciples and had to wash his feet. I mean, how could you even consider that such a thing might be do-able with a whole lot of schoolgirls?'

At St Mary's, Wantage in the early 1960s, piety was no laughing matter. When I asked Caroline Dawnay, 'What is the first thing you see when you think of St Mary's?' she said, 'A horrid lone conifer in the middle of The Circle in the drive.' And the second? 'The chapel.' Again, instantly we have the aura; and the lone conifer is a key part of it. Piety, plainness, shade. Here is Caroline's description of the Wantage chapel cap: 'It was like two pieces of A4 stuck together, made of starched linen, as stiff as boards but they bent a third of the way down. A ribbon was tied underneath the back of the head.' Wearing these caps, the girls processed in and out of chapel at least once a day for their various devotions. St Mary's was part of the Community of St Mary the Virgin, the largest collection of Anglican nuns in the world. 'Some were sent to work at St Catherine's, the local lunatic asylum, some were sent to Poona, and some ran St Mary's.'

Piety could be an anaesthetic for homesickness: Caroline was homesick and spent hour upon consoling hour in the chapel, singing psalms to Gregorian chant under the conducting of Sister Honor Margaret, and singing endless hymns: 'I know the whole of the English Hymnal by heart.' It was on coming out of Confession one day that she learned that President Kennedy had been assassinated.

The auras of the different schools worked their way under girls' skins and into their souls and could become hard to shake off – hence the fact that you can often tell which one a woman went to, decades later, when you spot her doing an errand on a London street. Foreigners find it hard to understand the British obsession with asking people 'Which school did you go to?' But, with such a gallery of varied eccentric institutions to choose from, we need to check whether our surmises are correct.

But what happened if parents chose a school with completely the wrong aura for their daughter? In those days of slapdash school-choosing, this happened. A clever girl could find herself bored stiff at a school where all anyone talked about was which dances they were going to in the holidays. Cynthia Colman remembers only being allowed to take one book per term to Southover, a school chosen by parents because they knew the other parents. 'I brought a book of Saki short stories, and it was confiscated.'

On the other hand, you could be an unacademic girl who had somehow scraped into Cheltenham. Then you might have to suffer the ignominy of staying on for a year after School Certificate, but not to do any more exams. You were put into the Citizenship Class – and that was 'the dregs'. Citizenship Class girls went on day trips to look round magistrates' courts, and no one took them seriously. So extreme was Cheltenham Ladies' College in the 1950s that it deserves its own chapter.

8

'May I tag?' Survival at Cheltenham

It was the stark contrast with their previous lives that really hit some girls when they arrived at Cheltenham Ladies' College in the 1940s and early '50s. Here are two experiences of transition from one world to the other.

Pat Doyne-Ditmas had been one of the only two girls at Winchester House, a boys' prep-school in Northampton-shire, allowed to go there because her father was headmaster. The teaching was excellent: this was a boys' school, so they were learning Latin and Greek grammar at the age of 8 and were doing deponent verbs by 11. Life in the classrooms was strict and high-achieving, but life in the corridors was relaxed and merry. 'We were just like boys,' said Pat. 'We took great runups and slithered along the oak corridors, as all the boys did. We ran up the staircases three steps at a time, chatting and laughing. It wasn't an unruly school – not at all: it was just that it was fine to slide in the corridors and chat on the stairs. None of the masters minded.'

When Pat went to look round Cheltenham with her mother in the term before going there in 1945, she couldn't think what was wrong with all the girls. 'There was complete silence throughout. Girls were walking silently along the corridors between lessons, looking as if they'd got rods up their backs. I couldn't think who all these strange, subdued figures were.'

The answer was that they were Cheltenham girls who knew it was more than their life was worth to be seen talking in the corridors or walking with a slouch. Talking was forbidden anywhere in College except in the classrooms at appropriate moments. You weren't even allowed to talk in the cloakrooms. Prefects were posted along corridors to police the silence, ready to pounce. No running was allowed except on the games field, and stairs had to be ascended one step at a time. Deportment marks were read out each week. No one wanted to lose points for her house.

'Pat Arrowsmith! Your knees!' Those words still shriek in Pat's ears seventy years later: she was not the Pat in question, but another girl, the future CND supporter and peace campaigner Pat Arrowsmith, was sitting with her knees slightly apart in the hall and was barked at by the headmistress Miss Popham (whose nickname, unsurprisingly, was 'Popeye').

*

We have already met Jennifer McGrandle, stagnating at the sweet but hopeless Ryton Hall with its thistly games field and two-shelf library. When she arrived at Cheltenham in 1949, she was dumbfounded to discover that two such violently different schools could exist on the same planet. A two-shelf library at Ryton Hall, an enormous, Gothic-style, high-ceilinged temple of books at Cheltenham, as well stocked as the library of an Oxbridge college, with bays, ladders, tables, lamps and girls buried deep in piles of books. 'There's *this* school, and there's *this* school,' the young Jennifer realized. But there was not much time for contemplation as the harsh daily routine was already under way. 'What are you doing walking on the furniture?' the mistress barked when Jennifer, in order to get to her place on the bench, tiptoed along the edge of it behind the backs of the already-seated girls. 'Do you do that at home?'

Again, as with the tooth-brushing incident at Badminton, we hear the cutting remark that makes a girl question her home life and her parents' method of bringing up children. In her first week Jennifer got into trouble for holding her pen incorrectly. But no one at Ryton Hall had ever told her how to hold her pen.

'One of my first Cheltenham reports,' Jennifer told me, 'said, "Jennifer is more of a liability than an asset." So I've always known the opposites of *those* two words.' We can imagine the mistress, her nib hovering over the report, honing those antonyms with relish.

*

So, two different kinds of contrast: from merry, chatty, corridor-slithering boy-world to subdued, ramrod-straight girl-world; and from gentle, academically aimless, stuck-away-in-the-middle-of-Shropshire world to bracingly harsh, intimidating world. Already, the aura of Cheltenham is building up: disciplined, eloquently sarcastic, cutting girls down to size. For some reason, in those days, there was a theory that in order for girls to acquire as good an education as boys (which had been Cheltenham's admirable aim ever since its founding in 1853), conditions needed to be harsh and pastoral care kept to a minimum.

To new girls the Ladies' College felt overwhelming like a cathedral: when you sat at your desk, the Gothic-revival windows threw Gothic-shaped shadows on your exercise books. The pictures to visualize when you think of Cheltenham are: girls holding their pens correctly over the Gothic shadows and trying not to shake as they wrote words that might well evoke a withering response in the marking; and girls walking backwards and forwards three times a day to and from their boarding-houses, which were spread out across the town, sometimes fifteen minutes' walk away. All meals were in the houses. For deportment purposes, the regulation canvas sacks of books with leather handles had to be carried on the right shoulder on Mondays, Wednesdays and Fridays and on the left shoulder on Tuesdays, Thursdays and Saturdays.

You might think those walks through the town at least gave girls a dose of freedom and independence, but they didn't. For one thing, there was a map in the College showing which roads you were allowed to walk along. The streets marked in green were permitted; the streets marked in red were out-of-bounds: those were the streets the boys from the Boys' College were allowed to walk on. Never must girl meet, or even glimpse, boy. The girls were allowed on the Promenade but not on the High Street; and vice versa for the boys. This rule even held when you were with your parents. Visiting fathers thought it absurd that they weren't allowed to take their daughters out to tea in a High Street tea-shop; but the daughters said, 'Really – please don't – there are perfectly good tea shops on the Promenade.'

For another thing, you were never allowed to walk through the town on your own: you had to be in groups of at least two. On the first day of term girls said 'Will you be my partner on Monday mornings?' and 'Will you be my partner on Wednesday lunchtimes?' and so on. But some girls – and this explains the title of this chapter – did not have enough friends to walk with, and sometimes did not have any friends at all. They had to say, 'May I tag?' The tagging girl – Anne Hancock was one of them, and has never quite got over it – had to walk a few steps behind the pair of friends. 'It has given me a lifelong insecurity about belonging,' said Anne. Lugging her heavy sack uphill – her house, Glenlee, was a mile away, up near the vast games fields – she looked at the confident, striding backs of the pair of friends in front of her and felt desolate.

The town was full of spies: an ogling network of old ladies

who had been girls at the College themselves, so knew if you weren't wearing the right hat elastic. 'They would ring up the housemistress and report you,' Anne said. So, not much freedom while you walked.

It didn't take girls long to work out that they needed to find a strategy to survive at this place. You needed to carve some kind of niche for yourself; and you needed a trusted friend. Anne did find a friend, Susie Vereker, who saved her and invited her to stay in the holidays so she didn't always have to go to 'Auntie Gladys and Uncle Tom' in Walton-on-Thames.

Life at Cheltenham was a constant search for kudos. There was a pecking-order, and those at the bottom gazed up in wonder at those at the top. By accident of birth or house-placement or athletic ability, you were in or out. Pat Doyne-Ditmas was surprised to acquire some kudos in her first week. She happened to be good at cricket for two reasons: she had been at a boys' school where cricket had been well taught, and, more importantly, her mother, Joan Thomas, played cricket for England. There was a cricket net in the garden at home and Pat had had ample time to copy her mother's batting technique.

'I was amazed by how hopeless the Cheltenham girls were at batting when I arrived,' said Pat, 'tossing the ball about.' Aged 82 and looking not a day over 60, she stood up in my kitchen and imitated a Cheltenham girl tossing a ball into the air with a bat in an ethereal, ladylike, lightly bouncing way. 'I'd been well trained and came *forward* to the ball,' she demonstrated. 'On my first cricket afternoon the games mistress, Miss Tandy, came up to me in her divided skirt and said, "Are you a relation of Thomas, by any chance?" My mother was so well-known in the world of women's cricket that she was known by her surname. Miss Tandy had recognized my mother's batting style. "I've seen her at the Oval!" she said; and I got straight into the first team, at the age of 12. That was the only thing that gave me any kudos at all.'

Anne Hancock wasn't much good at cricket because she had been evacuated to a lovely school in Ottawa, Elmwood, where she had played baseball and learned to drop the bat. 'I found it difficult to lose that habit,' she said. She also declined the Latin noun *mensa* in the 'wrong' order (nominative, genitive, dative, accusative, ablative) – Canada followed the 'Continental system' for declensions – which meant that, although she was good at Latin, she was put into a low set.

Jennifer McGrandle's mother had been at the school: this gave Jennifer a modicum of acceptability. But she was badly diminished by the fact that when she started there she was a day-girl, 'and the sink house of all was the day-girls' house, simply known as "Day-girls". I loathed being a day-girl. We were regarded as the dregs. The boarders were a superior breed.'

In a school of 800 girls there were only 40 day-girls;

they had their own common room in the main part of the College. 'On the first day, I remember a jolly girl called Caroline Gordon-Walker going round all the new girls asking us what houses we were in.' Instantly each new girl was 'placed': the tops, the pits or somewhere in between. The girls with high social connections tended to be in St Hilda's. The girls who were good at games and in the teams were in St Margaret's. They were the most admired girls in the school, although there was a pecking order of games teams: to be in the fencing team did not rank as high as being in the hockey First XI.

Miss Popham favoured the high-born and the well-connected girls. The head girl was Colette Clark, Kenneth Clark's daughter. Anne and Susie's house, Glenlee, was very low in the pecking order. It was a house in which to put girls whose parents lived in far-flung corners of the Empire.

We'll hear more about the ruthless way girls can size one another up in a later chapter, but Cheltenham was a place where everyone knew what everyone else's fathers did, and this also created a pecking order. 'To have a father who was a doctor or a surgeon was fine,' said Jennifer McGrandle. 'The very comfortable girls were the ones who came from the Cheshire green belt, with professional parents, high up in some kind of bank. There was one girl whose father was the theatre critic of the *Sunday Times* – these were the things one knew. I can remember a girl whose father was believed to be a builder's merchant in Wales. I mean, that was just the bottom.'

Rosie de Courcy told me that one of the reasons her parents sent her to Lawnside rather than Cheltenham was that (as they saw it) 'Cheltenham was full of doctors' and dentists' daughters.' 'Lots of the girls were the daughters of consultants at big northern hospitals,' said Miranda Villiers, who went there in 1947 and was in the ultra-cool St Hilda's. 'John Moores's daughters were there – he ran Littlewoods Football Pools. There was a northern, top-of-the-A5 feeling about Cheltenham. It used to call itself "a girls' Winchester". It could never have called itself "a girls' Eton".'

These subtle (and sometimes not so subtle) social gradations show how locked into social snobbery Britain was in those days, and not just at Cheltenham. Girls were branded with what their parents did, and then branded later with which school they had been to: a whole life with labels on the forehead. There were racial labels too. Jennifer remembers the moment when the Scripture teacher mentioned a girl formerly at the College who was a Jew, 'and one of the girls in our class put her hand up and said, "She's my cousin!" We all gasped and thought, "You're a Jew, then!" The girl was compartmentalized from then on.' (Helen Holland and her sister suffered similar compartmentalization and isolation at St Bride's, Helensburgh because of their dark skin. 'Years later,' Helen said, 'I asked another Old Girl why we'd been so unpopular, and she said, "It wasn't that we didn't like you: we just didn't know what to do about your skin colour."')

Some girls thrived. Miranda Villiers admitted to me that she was enough of a typical aspiring schoolgirl to want to be a Cheltenham prefect. 'You're sitting next to someone who really *loved* the idea of boarding-school,' she told me. As a young girl she had immersed herself in girls' school stories and was swept away by the romance of boarding-school life. Miranda made it her business to be spotted and liked by Miss Popham and thus groomed for prefectship. Needless to say, there was a pecking order of prefects: at the bottom, House Prefects; then College Prefects, who read the lesson and had their own rooms; then Committee Prefects; then the Senior Prefect, 'who was God'. 'I did become a College Prefect for two terms, which I regarded as a great achievement. We had to direct the traffic when 800 were filing in to prayers.'

Miranda also ran one of the clubs, the Cotswold Club, with prefectorial strictness. 'Club members used to bicycle round the county looking at old churches. You had to pass an exam to get into the club: you had to know what an aumbry was, and so on. I did enjoy marking that exam.'

There were some terrifying women about. Miss Blandford, head of the lower school, was 'stout and ugly, with Eton-cropped hair', remembers Susie Vereker. 'She seemed ancient, though she was probably in her early fifties. I don't think I ever saw her smile. On my first day, she attacked me.'

'Attacked you?'

'Well, it was in the Lower Hall, which looked more like a church. A prefect took me in to see her. She didn't look up for a while. Then she got up from her chair and came round to face me. "Well, what would your parents think?" she asked. I wondered, "What on earth do you mean?" Then she started to poke me and pull at my clothes, with horrid angry eyes. I can only think now that she was a bit crazy. She wanted to dominate.'

With hindsight it's clear Miss Blandford was a bit crazy; but then, the mistresses' priority was to keep a lid on the girls' perceived craziness. 'They felt that if we stepped out of line – if we spoke to a boy or even looked at a boy – we might go crazy,' Susie said. 'Once, I did look at a choirboy in church and my house lady [the Cheltenham word for housemistress] Mrs Garner spotted it. She hauled me into her study and told me I wasn't allowed to say goodnight to her for the rest of term.'

'Not allowed to say goodnight to her?'

'We had to go into her study one by one every evening to say goodnight. You'd knock on the door and she would say, "Come!" Then she would say, "You haven't come in the right way. Go out and do it again." Then, "Goodnight, Mrs Garner." "Goodnight."'

It was a nightly ordeal; but being excluded from it made a girl feel banished. We see how a once-gentle convention of saying goodnight to your housemistress – a term-time replacement for your mother – could be twisted into a loveless, rule-ridden test of deportment.

There were other brutal women, such as 'Tigger', the gym mistress: 'Gosh, she bullied us,' said Susie. 'She made you do things that were painful, such as putting your head on the floor between your legs: she put her foot on my back to try to push me down.' The school nurses were an unsympathetic bunch. 'A friend of mine called Fleur had bad asthma,' said Susie, 'and the nurse just said, "Oh, Fleur, do stop that silly coughing." When I had appendicitis the nurse didn't take it seriously as I didn't have a temperature, although I was in agony. Luckily there happened to be a doctor visiting that morning, and he rushed me off to hospital.'

Jennifer McGrandle was asked to hand out test-papers to the whole of the class, but there weren't quite enough copies to go round. She told the teacher, and the teacher said, 'But I expect you've kept one for yourself?' This was a typically cutting, sarcastic remark, expecting the worst rather than the best from the pupils.

A thread of this emotional austerity ran through a succession of schools. Dame Frances Dove (1847–1942), an early Girtonian, became Assistant Mistress of Cheltenham in 1877, and then headmistress of St Leonards in 1882, before going south to found Wycombe Abbey in 1896. In 1923 three mistresses from Wycombe Abbey went off to found Benenden. At all these related schools, but particularly strongly at Cheltenham and St Leonards, it was frowned upon for any girl to draw attention to herself. Self-pity was not tolerated at these establishments, which modelled themselves on boys' public schools, where stoicism was expected.

Mary James, who was at St Leonards in the late 1950s, remembers that when one girl's father was killed in a car-crash, the girl went away for three days and then came back to school, 'and no one talked about it'. When she herself received a letter from home telling her that her dog had died, Mary spent the whole of lunch weeping, but nobody asked her why. '"Don't bore others with your emotions" was the unspoken rule,' Mary said. The emphasis was on sub-jugating the ego and giving service to others less fortunate than yourself. This didn't seem to apply to being nice to unpopular girls. One girl at Cheltenham had terrible acne and she always had to tag.

Life in the houses at Cheltenham was more relaxed than life in College: you were at least allowed to talk. But the houses weren't particularly cosy. Gloss paint was used for the bedroom walls. 'My first memory of St Hilda's house,' said Diana Copisarow, who went there in 1945, 'was the lavatory tiles on the wall going up the stairs.'

Miss Popham was a distant figure, elegant and well-dressed in a suit and pearls, with shiny shoes. She seemed to have a close friendship with Miss Davison, who ran the san and wore a nurse's uniform: they shared a dog, Peter, who was shown off to the parents. Pat Doyne-Ditmas only spoke to Miss Popham twice during her whole five years at the school – 'once when I'd foolishly taken a whole jar of "Sylph" slimming pills, hoping I'd wake up sylph-like, and Popeye had a strong word with me; and once when I went to see her before my Cambridge interview and all she said was, "When you get up to leave, you must remember to puff up the cushions." No mention of how I should talk about Aeschylus.'

The fact that Aeschylus was on Pat's agenda at all was a measure of the counterbalancing side of Cheltenham life. It educated girls ruthlessly but brilliantly. All the Old Girls I spoke to still appreciate the excellent education it gave them. 'If you could stand the light,' Miranda Villiers said, 'Cheltenham was a great and shining beacon in women's education.' This sentence from the 1952 school magazine – a sentence containing the magazine's sole exclamation mark – gives a glimpse of the typical level of attainment. Written by one of the girls, it describes a school outing to see the Bradfield Greek play, *Antigone*:

It took us some time to accustom ourselves to the old pronunciation of Greek, but the lines were so clearly and passionately declaimed that it was not difficult to follow, even without the help of Loeb!

At the back of that 1952 magazine, at a time when schools like Southover and Tudor Hall were given a day's 'whole holiday' if a single girl got into university, there are five pages of university achievements: twenty-three places at Oxford and Cambridge, eight places at London hospitals to train for Medicine, and twenty places at other universities.

'You weren't told you'd done well,' said Diana Copisarow. 'They just said, "We think you're finding the work too easy in this year, so we're moving you up." I longed to be praised: some children need a carrot, not a stick.' But at least the teachers were attuned to a girl's academic standard and were quick to act. 'If you loved Latin,' said Jennifer, 'they really took you *on*.' The Classics teacher was none other than Miss A. K. Clarke, author of *A History of Cheltenham Ladies' College* (1953), and she was a true bluestocking, 'a great brain on a little wizened body', said Miranda Villiers, 'with a strange "eh-teh" stammer'. When Miranda was about to be presented at Court in the 1953 Coronation Presentation, Miss Clarke said to her, 'If it's not too *banal* a question, what are you going to wear?'

If you read the small advertisements at the back of the 1952 Cheltenham magazine, you'll see that not all girls left in a blaze of academic glory. As well as 'For girls' schoolwear, there's nothing to equal Clydella', you find advertisements for secretarial colleges in London: St James's, St Godric's, Mrs Hoster's. These places were waiting for the second tier of girls who did the Citizenship Class. These girls, in that competitive environment, felt like failures.

The husband of their housemistress, Mrs Garner, was still a prisoner-of-war in Japan when Susie and Anne Hancock arrived as girls at Glenlee in 1944, and this, Susie thinks, accounts for some of her meanness: she was at her wits' end with worry. VE Day was no day of celebration for her. As with DW at Lawnside, we can and do feel pity for these women. Miss Popham retired to live a solitary life in a block of flats off Kensington High Street. Having been trained in service to others, Diana Copisarow, in middle age, did the decent thing and invited old Miss Popham to stay in Denham, where she and her family lived. 'I thought, "Poor old lady: she's blind and lonely", and I had a husband and children by then – she couldn't bully me, could she?"'

Diana drove old Miss Popham to the local chemist to buy some pills, and the blind old lady couldn't find the right coins in her purse. 'She was fumbling,' said Diana, 'so I dipped my fingers into her purse, to help her look for the coins. She gave me a smart slap.'

So Popeye still could be a bully. But at least Diana could no longer be summoned to her study for a rasping telling-off, as had happened when she was caught tidying the College library just after 9 p.m.

You might hope, after all this snobbery at Cheltenham – intellectual, sporting, ethnic and social – that the convent boarding schools of the next chapter would be egalitarian by comparison. But you would be wrong.

9

Teaching Nuns and Kitchen Nuns

How, in convent boarding-schools, did you tell the difference between teaching nuns and kitchen nuns? Easy. Teaching nuns had upper-class accents and glided through the convent with a Bible in one hand and a copy of *Debrett's Peerage* in the other. Kitchen nuns had Irish accents, squints, red hands from all the cooking and washing, and limps.

This is an exaggeration but not a total one: in some Catholic girls' schools that really was the case, and in most the truth was somewhere on that spectrum. At St Mary's, Ascot in the 1950s the high-born nuns hid the school's copy of *Debrett's* in a cupboard, rather than carrying it or keeping it in the school library, 'because', they said, 'we don't want the girls to know our ages'.

Often from aristocratic families themselves, they favoured titled parents. St Mary's, Ascot Open Days in the 1950s were so snobbish that tea was held in three separate venues: titled families in one common room, untitled families in another, and staff and working nuns in a third. At the other end of the social spectrum, the limping Irish kitchen nuns at the Franciscan convent in Taunton used to mutter, within earshot of the homesick 10-year-old Brigid Keenan as she walked along the corridor, 'There goes Brigid Keenan, doing the Devil's work on earth.'

What were nuns doing (a) running boarding-schools and (b) being snobbish? Well, they were running schools because the visionary nuns who founded their orders had themselves been educationalists. Mary Ward, who founded the Institute of the Blessed Virgin Mary in 1609, was an inspirational early women's libber who made outspoken comments such as 'Wherein are we so inferior to other creatures that they should term us "but women?"' St Madeleine Sophie Barat, who founded the Society of the Sacred Heart after the French Revolution, was an inspired educational delegator, setting in motion the birth of hundreds of Sacred Heart girls' schools that still exist around the globe. Woldingham in Surrey is one of them.

Mother Cornelia Connelly, Catholic convert and mother of five, founded the Society of the Holy Child Jesus in the 1840s and started Mayfield in East Sussex in 1863. Mère Marie Eugénie Milleret, who founded the Order of the Assumption in 1893, wanted girls to grow up as intellectual equals to the men they would marry, and thus able to defend their arguments for bringing their children up to be good Catholics.

The snobbishness is harder to explain. As we have seen, it seems to be a foible of mid-twentieth-century boarding-school headmistresses that they had a weakness for 'good' families, and particularly for their handsome fathers, who wore overcoats made by the very best London tailors. You would think nuns might be above (or at least removed from) such snobbery, but they could in fact be some of the worst culprits. Perhaps it was partly that, having given up their earthly possessions and devoted their whole lives to the community, and having removed all signs of their own backgrounds from their appearance and dress, they needed to cling harder than others to the psychological trappings of good society, and needed to show the world that they were still in the know about titles and castles.

Also, having countless hours for silent contemplation, they had leisure to let their thoughts roam freely over the delicious and (to them) endlessly fascinating subject of grand Catholic family trees. There were only a handful of Catholic recusant families in Britain – quite a small 'pool' – and the headmistress wanted to be sure that *her* school secured the daughters of these families. Once she acquired one sibling a large retinue of younger sisters would follow, and one more glamorous Catholic surname on the register would attract other grand families to apply. The last thing the headmistress wanted was to have to go downmarket and open the doors to a flood of Irish girls.

Mother Bridget, headmistress of St Mary's, Ascot from 1956 to 1976, relished her position as Chooser of Suitable Catholic Girls. As well as bagging the 'top' English Catholic families, she managed to put St Mary's on the map as *the* place for foreign royal and presidential families to send their Catholic daughters. So the Spanish infantas went there, and President Marcos's daughters, and Princess Caroline of Monaco, and Mother Bridget was 'all over them like a rash', Old Girls recall. Thanks to this careful social engineering, and because recusant families intermarried for generations, Catholic girls' boarding-schools such as St Mary's, Ascot, Woldingham, St Mary's, Shaftesbury and Mayfield were stuffed full of cousins. Whenever I hear the names of female saints reeled off at lightning speed by the priest during the Eucharistic Prayer at the London Oratory – 'Felicity, Perpetua, Agatha, Lucy, Agnes, Cecilia, Anastasia and all your saints' – I can't help imagining these haloed figures as cousins who were at St Mary's, Ascot together. At a typical St Mary's lunch there would be about forty of one's cousins in the dining-room.

Mother Bridget taught Latin to the juniors and she kicked off the first Latin lesson of the new 11-year-olds in 1976 with this ice-breaker: 'Now, hands up any of you whose house is open to the public.' 'Quite a few hands did go up,' remembers Maggie Fergusson, 'and this started a chat about a few of the girls' stately homes, before we started doing any Latin.' If you weren't lucky enough to come from a family that opened its house to the public, you were by no means a shoo-in for admission to the school. 'When my eldest sister Kitty came to look round,' Maggie said, 'it was pretty clear that Mother Bridget didn't think much of us as we actually *lived* in Ascot, which wasn't really good enough. She was saying to my mother, "Well, I can't promise that we have a place for your daughter ... " when one of the mothers with a big country house came into the school and flung her arms round my mother, as they were cousins. That changed everything. Mother Bridget said she would take Kitty after all.' If your parents were divorced, God help you: you had almost no chance of getting in.

Victoria Mather, who was at Woldingham in the 1960s, passed the social test: 'My grandmother paid my school fees,' she said. 'She was the Hon. Isobel Catto; her father Lord Catto was Governor of the Bank of England. Mother Shanley liked that. But she didn't like it when my mother went bankrupt, which she did several times.'

With nuns, also, we come across some of the most forthright political incorrectness and the most blatant right-wingness to be found in girls' boarding establishments. We must remember that many of the nuns had themselves been educated at the convent where they now taught, so they had hardly been in the outside world and were slow to catch up with the way things were going. The needlework nun at

St Mary's was a rigorous and wonderfully patient sewing teacher called Sister Mary Joseph. In the spring term the girls knitted clothes for the sister school in Chishawasha, Rhodesia. 'Black people look *much better* in brighter colours,' Sister Mary Joseph cheerfully told the girls. 'So we all chose the most garish colours we could find,' said Maggie Fergusson: 'pink, mango and mint-green.'

The teaching nuns' cut-glass accents still ring in the ears of girls who were at St Mary's in Mother Bridget's days. The word 'toilet' was forbidden. When a new girl shyly asked, 'Please may I go to the toilet?' Mother Bridget replied with disdain, 'NO girl *ever* goes to the toilet at this school.'

This, Maggie Fergusson told me, was how the Reverend Mother, Mother Isobel, addressed the girls when it became known that a man had escaped from Broadmoor psychiatric hospital ten miles away: 'Now, girls, should you meet this gentleman on your way back through the woods from the junior house, this is what you should do. If he initiates a conversation, you should simply join in and agree with him. So, if he says, "I am the Queen of Sheba", you should reply, "Yes, you are the Queen of Sheba". But if he doesn't initiate a conversation, you should say something perfectly natural to him, such as, "Are you a caddy from the *goff* course?"'

Mother Isobel happened to be Frank Muir's sister-in-law and she invited him to come and present the prizes at the end of the summer term. Muir opened his speech to the assembled parents, who included some of the Spanish Royal

Family, with the words, 'Your Majesty; Lords and Ladies; peasants.' 'That was about right,' said Maggie. With a twinkle in his eye and a memorable plumminess in his own voice, Muir had put his finger on the three social layers, as seen through Mother Bridget's eyes.

As for right-wingness, at Woldingham in 1963 the nuns had a Mass said for Alec Douglas Home to win the General Election. Artemis Cooper told her mother this and mentioned that the school had also had a visit from the local Conservative candidate. 'Did you have a visit from the Labour candidate?' her mother asked. 'Or the Liberal one, by any chance?' Artemis said 'No' – 'and that was *it* for my mother. I never went back.' From the sheltered Conservative world of the convent – a world in which it was conveyed to a girl by osmosis that (a) if you weren't Catholic you'd go to Hell and (b) all Russians were evil and wanted to blow up the world, Artemis was propelled into the contrasting world of Camden School for Girls, where she nearly fainted with shock when girls in her class told her they were Communists, and went around with Chairman Mao's *Little Red Book*.

The girls at the Assumption Convent, evacuated from Ramsgate to Herefordshire during the war, were told by the nuns to pray for a Conservative victory in 1945, Catherine Freeman said, 'because they were worried that if the Labour party got in, they might be shot'. Mad though this seems, one can see the logic of it: the Order of the Assumption was a French order and many of the Belgian and French nuns were remembering the Spanish Civil War when some of their sisters had in fact been shot.

At the Assumption Convent the two strata of nuns were the Choir Nuns and the Lay Sisters. They wore different habits and prayed in different languages. The Choir Nuns wore full-length purple habits with full skirts which they kilted up over black overskirts 'in a becoming eighteenth-century manner', Catherine Freeman said, and they prayed in Latin. The Lay Sisters wore simple black-and-white habits and prayed in the vernacular.

The Lay Sisters did all the chores. Among Catherine's blissfully happy memories of the evacuated years in rural Herefordshire is the image of Sister Ubertina, peeling potatoes outside the kitchen door and talking to the French-named cats, Gris-Gris and Ti-Ti. It was made clear to the girls by the Reverend Mother that their exquisite school uniform (double-breasted fawn gabardine coat with white silk scarf, worn over a saxe-blue serge skirt and collared jersey from Daniel Neal in London) had been designed so that they would never, ever, be mistaken for local grammar-school girls.

Born into sprawling Catholic families of eight or nine siblings, of whom 'the plain, thick ones' (as Ann Leslie rather frankly put it) 'were put into the nunnery', the lowly working nuns laboured away unpaid to the end of their days, and, mostly, they were loved and thanked. Girls put out their dirty clothes in the passage and a few days later, back they all came, washed, ironed and folded in neat piles with each girl's name on top, finished to perfection by the working nuns.

As no one needed to find them a salary, they could be kept going for years with a single, tiny, repetitive daily duty. At St Mary's, Ascot in the mid-1970s, Sister Philomena's sole job was to make sure the girls tipped their glasses upside down on to a plastic tray at the end of lunch. She was 95. At the same convent in the 1950s, one working nun's job was simply to open the door to visitors. She was 'the Porteress'. When she died, the girls were taken down to the crypt to see her dead body laid out. Francesca Wall has never forgotten that. 'She looked as if she was asleep. We'd seen our first dead body by the age of 10. A good and wise lesson.'

Sister Camillis at St Mary's, Shaftesbury drove the tractor round and round the walled garden and organized a bonfire tea for the Lower Fourth on Saturday afternoons. She sold bath-cubes in the dispensary, ploughing all profits back into the community. 'My favourite nuns,' said Virginia Coates, 'were Sister John and Sister Felicity, two sisters from a family of eight: three or four had become nuns and two priests. Sister Felicity was tiny and gorgeous. She had developed a love of Alpine things: she made her music-room look like a little Austrian chalet. She recorded birdsong on a cassette player. Sister John ran the sewing-room and was always on hand to show you how to do a French seam. We cut out endless patterns – we were really churning out the clothes. Then there was Sister Anthony, who ran the tuck shop. She was also tiny and had apparently been "the Belle of Dublin" before becoming a nun. She drove a Mini: you could barely see her above the steering wheel.'

Unpaid, disciplined, early-rising and resident, nuns were ideally suited to running schools. They had infinite time to mark essays and prepare lessons, and infinite time to check every single girl's weekly sewing output. With each batch of girls they could hope to form a new generation of devoutly Catholic wives and mothers. The fees helped to keep the community going, and the girls, as we shall see, did some of the housework.

Convent schools were wrapped in a secure embrace by the presence of nuns who were themselves wrapped in the embrace of their daily offices and prayers. If a school like St Felix, Southwold exuded a sense of ceremonial calm, giving Tanya Harrod a lifelong nostalgia for gentle order and enclosure, convent schools did so perhaps even more. It was written into the timetable, and part of life, that the girls went on 'pilgrimages' round and round the games field in the pouring rain, holding white lilies and chanting '*Immaculata, Immaculata, ora pro nobis*', and that they sang the *Salve Regina* every Sunday evening beside a painting of the Madonna. At St Mary's, Ascot they stood up to say the Angelus on the dot of noon and 6 p.m. every day, even if they were in the middle of an exam. At their best, convents were reassuringly ordered, polished, calm, kind places.

The feeling of safety was one of the many things Artemis Cooper loved at Woldingham. 'I loved the grounds, I loved my cubicle with curtains round it, and I loved the nuns. I was fascinated by their habits: stiff white starch round their faces like blinkers and over that a black veil – white for novices. A long black habit with a pinafore, and a scapular-like cloak down to the waist, buttoned up. The nuns seemed so purposeful.' Convent girls, inspired by this purposefulness and regularity, have an inbuilt mental calendar of the liturgical rhythms of the year: the fasting of Lent, the feasting of Easter, and the countless saints' days. They still know the whole catechism by heart, all 369 questions and answers. You had to get even the punctuation exactly right in the catechism test.

'It was heaven,' said Catherine Freeman, remembering the safe, beautiful world of the evacuated Assumption Convent in Hereford (safe, apart, that is, from the fiendish Mother Ida whom we met in a previous chapter). The borrowed house, Belmont House, belonged to Major Wegg-Prosser, a kind Catholic who lent it, with its private chapel and extensive grounds, to the convent for the duration of the war. On the day of Catherine's arrival in September 1939 (the same day on which she had wiped away her tears with the ears of her toy rabbit in the train), the girls lined up on the gravel drive and were told by the headmistress to 'Cheer the Major, girls! Cheer the Major!' as he drove away in his car, not to be seen again till 1945.

'I remember the white violets in spring under the winter

hedges,' said Catherine, 'and the banks and banks of primroses. There was a proper Victorian long cultivated shrubbery. There were fields full of buttercups stretching steeply down to the River Wye. Because this was a French order, we had to speak French at meals and were encouraged to play French games in the garden, so the shrubbery was alive with sounds of *cache-cache*, and *loup, loup, que fais-tu?*' The school song, which Catherine can still recite, was temporarily inaccurate as it referred to the convent's Pugin-designed home in Ramsgate:

> *There's a peace and charm around us*
> *That no years may wear away,*
> *In this russet pile of buildings*
> *Looking out across the bay.*
> *Widespread art thou, fair Assumption,*
> *Great traditions hold us true ...*

'... and it goes on and on and gets more and more beautiful,' Catherine said rapturously. Singing that school song over and over again was one of the things that kept her going during three bouts of agonizing natural childbirth in the 1960s.

For the girls, part of the nuns' fascination was the near-disbelief that there were real human beings under those habits. Again, if secular schoolmistresses seemed so remote that no girl could imagine them having a bath or putting on a bra, how much more remote did nuns seem, whose femininity was almost completely hidden? If so much as a single wisp of hair escaped from the blinker-like circle of starch, girls would go into whispering raptures after lights-out. 'She's a redhead!' or 'She's a blonde!'

'We were obsessed by the nuns' physical appearance,' remembers Virginia Coates. 'We speculated endlessly, "If we took off your habit and dressed you in normal clothes, what would you look like?" In their habits the ugly ones and beautiful ones all looked the same.' In the junior dormitories at St Mary's, Ascot a nun slept in a cubicle near the door, just to keep an eye on things. A group of Old Girls I spoke to remembered stealing into their nun's cubicle during the daytime to try to get a glimpse of a pair of her pants.

It's the interface between nunliness and normality that convent girls remember vividly. It's the memory of a nun with her habit hitched up and her rosary beads rattling as she presided over a game of hockey, her ankles flashing in their black tights; or of a nun on a sit-up-and-beg bicycle doing errands round the grounds; or of a nun teaching ballroom dancing on a Saturday evening. Mother Currie at Woldingham 'taught the cha-cha-cha, the foxtrot and the Gay Gordons, with her robes billowing', said Artemis Cooper. Mother Oakshott, who gave the girls a spoonful of treacle-like Radio Malt when they queued up at the infirmary, 'wore round John Lennon glasses before John Lennon did'. Lisa Hiley remembers a slightly creepy moment at St Mary's, Ascot in the 1970s when a postulant called Sister

Julian said to her, 'Oh, you've got eyes just like your uncle George!' It turned out that Sister Julian had been a girl-friend of Lisa's uncle George in her previous life, and this was somehow too much information.

Presided over by the Reverend Mother, who was as remote as the Pope and almost as revered, the nuns lived in 'the nuns' part', separate from the school buildings, and this was a place of mystery and thus mystique: no pupil ever went in there. A girl once streaked across the lawn in front of the nuns' part at St Mary's, Ascot as a dare. 'If a girl was brave enough to do that,' her cousin said to me, 'she could run the country.' If you passed the Reverend Mother in the grounds, you had to do an instant, sweeping curtsey as you went by. Girls were made aware that they were cogs in the great wheel of the religious life: the nuns had whole prayer-ful lives apart from them. It was rumoured that at dead of night, after girls' lights-out, the Ascot nuns went swimming in the outdoor pool, but no girl ever saw this happen.

The girls were also useful cogs in the wheel of housekeep-ing. While some boarding-school women have red fingers from chilblains, Virginia Coates has red fingers from Briz, an ancient form of Ajax. 'We had to clean our own basins,' she said. 'After supper we had to do the washing-up on a weekly rota system, standing at a huge conveyor machine, stacking the filthy plates, with steam everywhere. Detention was cleaning the corridors or laying the tables for break-fast. There *were* a few cleaning ladies from the village. The cleaning ladies' room stank of cigarette smoke.' So, it turns out, there were four strata of domestics: working nuns, charladies, pupils and pupils in detention.

A short digression here on boarding-school girls as unpaid labour: I've never heard of boys at boys' schools having to do the cleaning or table-laying, although they did have to go out to the woods to gather logs. Domestic work was considered part of a girl's education – exemplified in this 1970s headmistress's report on Caroline Robertson at Hanford: 'Matron especially says that she owes a great debt to Caroline – for she has never failed to help in every way, and especially with unfailing help laying out the breakfast.' At the evacuated Queen Margaret's, York during the war, the girls had a choice of activities at 8.30 a.m.: either cricket in the nets or dusting. Angela Mackenzie chose dusting. Anne Heseltine remembers having to polish the bare boards of her dormitory at St Helen's, Northwood in the 1950s. Westonbirt girls of the 1970s used to rush outside after breakfast to play lacrosse, and then come back into the main building for their 'dom work' before lessons.

Each girl was assigned a daily domestic cleaning or dusting task. The St Mary's, Ascot girls in the 1970s had to clean their basins and rooms on the last day of term and turn their chairs upside-down on their desks, and a nun would come and check that all four upturned chair legs were spotlessly dust-free. At Downe House in the 1950s this domestic drudgery was dignified by the name of 'Housecraft'. 'Housecraft' was an actual lesson – part of the timetable. The girls had to dust the furniture, mop the floors and clean the windows.

Considering that Downe House was an extremely snobby school in those days, full of titled girls who had never had to do any such thing at home, this is perhaps surprising, but the idea was that 'You mustn't ask the housemaid to do a job if you yourself don't know how it's done.' At Hatherop Castle in the 1970s the girls had to wash their own underwear with Stergene and dry it in a freezing attic with broken windows. If you hang up a pair of pants in those conditions they don't dry, they just turn to damp, frozen cardboard, as Georgina Petty discovered. 'You had to break off the ice, re-wash them and give them another squeeze. Sometimes it took a whole week for a pair of knickers to dry in winter.'

Woldingham in the 1950s had its fair share of Latin American diplomats' daughters and European aristocracy. 'The headmistress,' Ann Leslie remembers, 'was a crashing snob, terribly taken with rich aristocratic families.' Ann remembers these girls as 'exotic creatures who menstruated far earlier than we did because they'd been eating loads of meat since the cradle'. She also remembers the cries and sobs that rang along the corridors when one of them received the news that they had been affianced to a neighbouring landowner's son in Argentina or Peru.

What with the Spanish infantas and Irene Marcos at St Mary's, Ascot together, there needed to be two sets of body-guards patrolling the grounds. In an overwhelmingly female environment these bodyguards stood out. 'The Filipino ones looked like kung-fu warriors,' Mary Miers remembers. 'The Spanish bodyguards would come up against the Filipino bodyguards in the middle of the night, and each lot would think the others were intruders and put in urgent calls to their respective embassies.' There was one female Filipina bodyguard, and she had a special skill: when the girls won coconuts at the fair, she knew how to karate-chop them open with the side of her hand.

Apart from the bodyguards, the only man at St Mary's, Ascot in the 1970s was Needham, the odd-job man. A visiting priest was needed to say Mass, but the girls hardly saw his face: he was a tiny Franciscan friar who scuttled along to say Mass facing the altar, then went into breakfast with the nuns and scuttled away again. At St Mary's, Shaftesbury in the 1970s the priest, Father Egan, was resident and lived above the cleaning-ladies' room. A hero of Arnhem with a festering leg, he was 'worshipped' by the nuns, who wheeled a sumptuous feast to him on a trolley after Mass, which he ate alone in a lobby off the chapel.

Being devotedly devout didn't make the nuns any nicer or less nice than they would have been anyway. A woman's character will out, whatever the holy clothing and whatever the daily prayer-quota. Some were lovely and generous-spirited. Reverend Mother Rita of the Assumption told the 9-year-old Catherine Freeman to 'live dangerously', an instruction that Catherine took to heart and that inspired her for life. Mother Bridget at St Mary's, Ascot did not approve of girls living dangerously, or certainly not on Saturday afternoons during term-time in the 1960s. An enterprising girl called Maria Noel found the telephone number of a local ice-cream firm and arranged for its ice-cream van to park at the edge of the wood on a Saturday afternoon. The girls ran to the edge of the wood by the lane (just out of bounds) and had a delightful half-hour buying and eating ice-creams. Mother Bridget found out, and punished the girls by making them miss the only film of the term.

The nuns at the Franciscan convent in Taunton could be callously playful with the girls' deepest fears. 'The art nun told us ghost stories in the evenings,' said Brigid Waddams, 'fourteen of us boarders, doing our embroidery as we listened to her. The stories were terrifying – all about seeing the devil's face pressed against the window at night.' Because Brigid occasionally wet her bed with fright and homesickness she was put into an empty dormitory with thirty beds in it, and was frightened to death. 'I'm still a very scared person at night,' she told me. 'I can't be in a room with the curtains not closed in the dark.'

Some of the less well-educated nuns at the Presentation Convent in Matlock were particularly nasty. 'They made a girl called Lorraine stand on the desk, and beat her legs, when she got the Latin answers wrong,' said Ann Leslie. 'They were either cow-like or actively sadistic. They were puritanical – even talking about sanitary towels was considered depraved. They thought I was depraved because I'd had ayahs at home. I suppose, looking back, it must have been pretty awful for them, being sent away from their families in Ireland to be brides of Christ.' Ann was overjoyed to change schools at the age of 15 from the 'horrible dank prison' of Matlock to the kind world of Mayfield, where girls were encouraged to ask questions during lessons.

10

The Peaks and Troughs of Lessons

It's slightly shameful that I have taken this long to address the important question of what boarding-school girls learned in their classrooms. Aren't schools meant to be, first and foremost, places of academic learning? But in terms of hierarchy of memories, this chapter is positioned in about the right place. When I asked Old Girls to shut their eyes and tell me the first image of boarding-school life that came to mind, not a single one mentioned a classroom or a lesson.

In a way, that's one of the best things about boarding-schools: the dormitory life is so full of colour and incident that lessons seem a mere daytime sideline to get you through to the important matter of giving a bath-cube to your best friend for her birthday, putting a love-note on your pash's pillow, and stocking up for the midnight feast. Even for

Cheltenham girls, lesson memories came about fourth, after rules, the longing for popularity, and games.

This chapter, of all chapters, is going to be the one with the widest spectrum. At one end, lessons were hushed and terrifyingly high-powered. The teacher stood behind her desk and spouted information which must be learned, and grammar and formulae which must be mastered. Clever Cheltenham girls of the 1950s were prepared for Oxford and Cambridge by efficient teachers who wrote withering things like this.

I asked you for your account of these events, not Professor Bury's, which I am quite well able to read for myself. Read him by all means, and other authorities as well, but write your essay from your own know-ledge and in your own words. Your slavish reliance on the history book has meant that you have stopped far too soon. Bury may not have a chapter entitled 'The Peloponnesian League from 550–500 BC', but there is plenty to be said on the subject, and you should have had the initiative to think of it and say it. A disappoint-ing essay from one of your ability. C+

That was Miss Boggis, at the bottom of Pat Doyne-Ditmas's essay of 1949 (she was 15), and Pat is still blushing from the shame. She hastened to tell me that it was the only C she'd ever got. Pat didn't do 'Highers' (A-levels) – but this was not for the usual girls'-boarding-school reason that they were considered too difficult. On the contrary, they were considered too easy. Top Cheltenham classicists soared far above Highers and aimed straight for the Oxbridge entrance exam. Miss Biddle and Miss Yonge ('Biddle and Sponge'), the Classics teachers, gave the girls a deep knowledge, and through that a lasting love, of the way the Latin and Greek languages worked.

At the other end of the spectrum there was pitifully little ambition in the classroom, the decibel level was high and discipline was lacking. A small distraction, such as the sound of horses' hooves on the gravel drive, could send a whole class rushing outside to see what was happening, the teacher unable to stop them.

This happened at Hatherop Castle when the hunt came past one Wednesday. Lizie de la Morinière, who was one of the girls who ran out, told me that she had never finished a single piece of prep during her five years there. 'I stopped working at the age of 11 and I've never really worked since,' she said. She wandered out of a geography lesson one day and came back at the end, and no one noticed she'd been missing. Girls at schools at this end of the academic spectrum could leave school with no O-levels, no A-levels and precious little academic knowledge. They had to rely on their natural intelligence to survive. Think of Diana, Princess of Wales, who left West Heath in 1977 with a great deal of gumption and empathy for people but without a single O-level. How was that allowed to happen?

As I discovered when talking to girls who had been at such schools, you were simply allowed to give any subject up as soon as it became at all hard. 'I gave up Maths before O-level,' Laura Lonsdale told me – she was at West Heath at the same time as Lady Diana Spencer. 'I just let it slip, and no one paid any attention.' This system of giving up made the teachers' lives much easier: they never had to force girls through subjects they hated.

'I gave up Maths at 13,' said Rowena Saunders, who was at Hatherop in the 1960s. 'You only had to do it for the first year. It was such fun giving things up!' But she went on to say, 'I got no O-levels or A-levels. I wasn't educated, basically. It was terrible.' Bolla Denehy, who had a lovely time at Heathfield in the 1970s, came out with five O-levels and they didn't include Maths. 'Now I really regret that I wasted my education,' she said. 'There was no incentive. I can't think how my parents tolerated it. *Such* a waste of money.' Alexandra Etherington, who was also at Heathfield, loved the school and has 24 godchildren, told me that when she was there in the 1970s only three girls out of thirty in her year passed History O-level. She herself retook her Maths O-level but still didn't pass.

Why didn't the parents complain? A few did, gently: 'My mother was shocked by my lack of general knowledge,' said Aurea Carter, who was at West Heath in the 1950s, 'and she asked the school to teach us more.' But most parents had no idea what their daughters were learning, and didn't care, as long as they were being instilled with good manners and kindness and were making suitable friends. The brothers of these girls were being excellently educated at Eton and Harrow, writing Latin verse and doing equations ranging from simultaneous to quadratic, while their sisters were being asked exam questions such as:

> What type and quantity of material would you buy for a petticoat with a brassière top to be worn with a white organdie blouse? Sketch the 'lay out' of the pattern and show how you would decorate the petticoat with some form of embroidery.

That was an O-level Domestic Science question from 1952. It was kept by a St Elphin's, Darley Dale Old Girl. Actually, Domestic Science was frowned on at both academic extremes of the girls'-boarding-school spectrum for different reasons: at Cheltenham, because it was considered too low-brow, and at the posher schools because it was deemed unnecessary for later life. Why would you ever need to learn to cook? The headmistress of St Helen's, Northwood told Josephine Boyle's mother in 1950, 'I've never needed to boil an egg, and I don't think your daughter will ever need to either.' ('And I've been boiling eggs ever since,' Josephine told me.)

An English exam question set to the Hanford 12-year-olds in 1972 was, 'Explain, as carefully as you can, how you would lay the table for lunch at home.' There was still an ingrained idea, lingering from the early years of girls' education, that braininess in a female was not an attractive trait and that stretching girls intellectually could be dangerous. When Frances Dove founded Wycombe Abbey in 1896 she had to assure parents that 'the hours of study will be strictly limited'. It was feared that an intellectually taxing education could drive a girl mad as well as decrease her eligibility.

Lady Florence Craye's undesirability, in P. G. Wodehouse's *Jeeves Takes Charge*, is summed up by the fact that she makes Bertie Wooster plough through *Ten Types of Ethical Theory* and then tries to move him on to Nietzsche. Bertie describes Honoria Glossop in *The Inimitable Jeeves* as 'one of those dashed large, brainy, strenuous, dynamic girls you see so many of these days. She had been at Girton, where, in addition to enlarging her brain to the most frightful extent, she had gone in for every kind of sport and developed the physique of a middle-weight catch-as-can wrestler.' Those two female specimens could be caricatures of the Cheltenham girl and the Roedean girl respectively. Far safer to send your daughter to a gentle school where her femininity would not be threatened.

The headmistress of Hanford wrote this at the end of the 13-year-old Amanda Graham's report in 1972:

> This report proves that you have chosen the right school – she can't stand pressure – and does good work when she feels 'safe'. I am glad she got in to Newton Manor – she ought to work and take her 'O' levels – later rather than earlier – and she will be all right.

'We have super lessons today,' Amanda wrote in a letter home to her parents that same year. 'Reading, handwork, handwork, then the rest of the day is free and <u>TV</u> which is super.' Super indeed. Hanford was a wonderfully happy school. But Amanda got 29 per cent in the History exam and still managed to come third in the class. Newton Manor, the next school she went to, turned out to be 'failing and useless', so she went on to Croft House ('hopeless'). She managed to get one A-level, and was the only girl at the school even to try.

Schoolgirls are ruthless, and if a teacher allows the smallest chink to appear in her armour, they will home in on it and go for the kill. This was one reason why many of 'the Misses' at places like Beaufront, Cheltenham, Wycombe Abbey, Benenden, Badminton and Malvern Girls' College were so iron-hard, strict, humourless and covered in tweed during lessons: they were determined to keep their armour on and hold the lid down on any potential outbreak of mockery.

The weaker teachers were found out, and their teaching hours could be made hellish. One teacher at Hatherop in the 1960s spent a whole term in tears because the girls were so cruel to her. Another at Heathfield had a bucket of water tipped over her from the top of the classroom door every single morning. 'The teachers probably felt very bullied,' admitted Bolla Denehy. 'We were a very powerful year.'

At St James's, West Malvern in the 1950s, Fiona Buchanan and Margaret Redfern remember the whole class shutting the 'zany' Art teacher Mabel Varley (M. I. V., nicknamed 'Vim') into the pitch-dark epidiascope room. 'We used to walk into her class backwards wearing all our clothes backwards,' they said. A girl called Sue Burder took the fuses out of the fuse-box so the poor feeble Geography teacher, who taught in a tin hut near the stables, found her hut plunged into gloom in mid-lesson. At St James's, you could be moved up to a higher class, but this was a reward for good behaviour rather than for good work.

Schools like St James's seem old-fashioned now when you hear about them, but they actually thought they were modern and up-to-date. One of the 'modern' ideas at St James's, and at Cranborne Chase too, in the late 1940s and early '50s, was to introduce the Dalton System. This American-designed educational system involved giving pupils a week to complete a number of 'assignments', leaving them free to decide for themselves when to do them. It was meant to help with self-motivation and for some, it did. Caroline Cranbrook, who was at Cranborne Chase in the late 1940s, benefited greatly from this style of self-motivated working which prepared her for university life. 'The teachers were exceptional,' she said, and she can still recite reams of Lamartine and Musset. 'We saw our tutor every three weeks.'

This university-style education was thrilling. But for the less motivated it was a disaster. Girls simply didn't do any work at all from Monday to Thursday and then did the bare minimum on Friday, by which time it was too late.

St James's tried to counteract this tendency by awarding a whole free day to those who finished quickly, but it didn't do the trick. 'I didn't bother to work at all,' said Margaret Redfern.

At Cheltenham, meanwhile, there was no Dalton nonsense. Girls sat in silent rows, taking notes about declensions and tenses (if they were in the classical stream) or cell walls and nuclei (if they were hoping to train for medicine) as the teachers spoke or dictated. They were not expected to talk except when asked a question. There were no discussions or enthusiastic contributions. A teacher could suddenly get a bee in her bonnet about something and go on about it, and the girls just had to sit and take notes. Miss Popham, for example, during a Scripture lesson on the First Book of Samuel, went on and on about how the Philistines' foreskins were cut off and put into sacks. The girls at the receiving end of this long lecture have never forgotten it. Many of them were not even sure what a foreskin was. But they wrote it all down and learned it, often in quite a panicky way, for fear of withering comments at the bottom of their essays and low percentages in exams.

The Wycombe Abbey girls, too, were slaving away diligently. Michaela Reid was so terrified of 'Polly' (Miss Pollard, the Latin teacher), that she learned her Latin by torchlight after lights-out, and also clandestinely learned it during French lessons with the much less scary Miss Ratcliffe ('Ratty'). 'Polly kept the windows wide open during lessons, even in winter, and we had to get up every fifteen minutes and jump up and down and fling our arms around. She *made* us learn. We all got As.' Thanks to Miss Partridge ('Part'), the Scripture teacher, Michaela is well acquainted with the obscurer books of the Bible. Miss Partridge whispered the name 'Yahweh' in a voice hushed with reverence for the God of the Old Testament.

Now we come to the question I mentioned in the introduction to this book, the question that summed up a school's modernity and academic ambition in the midtwentieth century: how many Bunsen burners were there? In other words, how was the science teaching? As you can imagine, it varied. When Penrhos College was evacuated to Chatsworth during the war and the 'chemi-lab' was put into the stables with a 240-volt power supply, 'work of distinction' was done in there, according to the Inspector for Education. On the other hand, when I asked the group of 1960s Hatherop Castle girls whether their school had had a lab in those days, they gave me a blank look. 'A laboratory?' I expanded, hoping to jog their memories. 'Oh, *that* kind of lab!' one of them said. 'I thought you meant a Labrador.'

The answer was 'No'. No science, and no Latin. One of the Hatherop girls, Sarah Douglas-Pennant, told me that she had managed to get five O-levels and was considered a genius. ('If you weren't listening,' she said, 'you could easily never quite find out what the set texts were.') Lizie de la Morinière said she had still never, ever seen a test-tube and had no idea what a Bunsen burner was. The St Mary's, Wantage girls of the 1970s had only one Bunsen-burner memory, and that was of the time when they stole a chicken from the school kitchen and roasted it on a Bunsen burner. It took all night.

At Heathfield 'science began and ended with the Bunsen burner', said Camilla Geffen, who was there in the 1970s. 'For most of us,' said Rosie Stancer, 'science never got divided into Physics, Chemistry and Biology.' Scientific parents who wanted their daughters to be good at science might send them to Roedean, as Roedean did divide the sciences up into three separate subjects and had rows and rows of Bunsen burners in well-appointed labs.

If there was any biology at the more ladylike schools of the 1940s and '50s, it tended to be very much of the botanical variety. One of the most useful bits of knowledge Angela Mackenzie took with her from Queen Margaret's, York evacuated to Castle Howard, was an extensive knowledge of varieties of wild flower. 'There was a wild-flower test at the end of the summer term,' she said: A hundred types of wild flower lined up in a hundred test-tubes, and you had to say which they all were.' She has passed this lesser-stitchwort knowledge on to her sons and it has enhanced every country walk since. I like to think of the mistresses going about early in the morning on wild-flower test day, heads bowed down as they search for a specimen of all one hundred varieties.

*

At Cheltenham, you either did a great deal of science or hardly any. If you were in the science stream it was non-stop Bunsen burners and test-tubes, while if you were in the classical, modern languages or historical stream you just did one science lesson a week, nicknamed 'science for the bright girls'. 'I did no real science after the age of 12,' said Diana Copisarow. 'The last experiment in a science lesson I ever did was to put a parrot with a weight on its tail on to a chimneypiece.'

To which I replied with the obvious (but, I now see, rather dense) question, 'Did the parrot fall off?'

'No!' said Diana. 'That was the whole point!' The last experiment Pat Doyne-Ditmas remembers doing at Cheltenham, before being sucked into the classical stream, was looking at an amoeba through a microscope. 'Shamefully,' she said, 'my knowledge of science is mainly confined to the pre-Socratic (*c.* 600 to 500 BC). I do know, though, that the word "atom" comes from the Greek word meaning "indivisible". But even that bit of scientific knowledge is out of date.'

There was, it has to be said, a lot of deadly-dull teaching across all the schools: teaching by tired women in cardigans, many of them not university-educated themselves, who had been teaching the same lesson on the same day of the year from the same out-of-date textbooks for the past thirty years and didn't get out enough, so were not refreshed by new experiences or new thoughts. Lessons at St Mary's, Wantage in the 1970s were 'appalling – useless', said Georgina Petty, 'with waffly teachers. You didn't even know which subject they were trying to teach you.' 'I don't think we were being stretched at all,' said Cynthia Colman, who was at Southover in the early 1950s. 'We were just passing time till we left school.' One of the few lessons the Southover Old Girls could remember was when the science teacher 'went pink while describing the life-cycle of the amoeba.'

Postwar St Helen's, Northwood is a typical example of a school where lessons were decent enough but somehow dull and dulling. The fact that the school was in a dreary, built-up bit of Middlesex surrounded by golf courses didn't help. Anne Heseltine was uninspired. 'The two teachers I had weren't up to preparing people for university. One of them didn't concentrate on the subject: she was always straying off. My father used to send me to France on my own, as the only hope of learning French. The headmistress was very excited one day, announcing, "We're terribly lucky to have our new teacher who is *Cambridge-educated!*"' St Helen's was uninspiring enough if you were in the top stream; if you were in the lower stream, known euphemistically as 'The Parallel', there was even less ambition for you: no Latin or Chemistry at all, and more Art, Sewing and Domestic Science.

Jane Goddard, likewise, remembers the thrilling moment when two *young* Oxford graduates came to teach at Tudor Hall while it was evacuated to Burnt Norton, dramatically lowering the average age of the teachers. 'We all fell in love with Helen Bannatyne, who taught History. We all got honours in our School Certificate, thanks to her. The other one, Miss Durrant, was very left-wing. She asked me, in the first lesson, "What do you think the word 'freedom' means?"'

'Erm – being able to do what you like?' replied Jane.

To which Miss Durrant let out a tirade. 'She was withering and made me feel I'd never had a thought in my life. "WHAT would it be like if we all drove on the same side of the road? Freedom must be limited to be possessed." That really woke me up. Those two young teachers had an amazing effect on us.'

But all too often the old cardiganed teachers droned on and on for years, not replaced by younger ones. At Beaufront, 'Miss Fleming taught History and didn't know any,' said Amanda Vesey, 'and Mrs Gainsford's sister taught Music but had no music in her, poor woman. She banged the piano and shouted at us.' Bice Crichton-Miller ('Bice' pronounced 'Beechy') at Sherborne School for Girls in the early 1970s had been at the school herself and was 'a wise old boot', said Anna Hamer, 'with terrible arthritis, hobbling around. She was good at history herself but had no clue how to help someone like me who was no good at exams. She gave me two out of ten for my history homework but could never explain how I might improve.'

At St Elphin's, Darley Dale in the 1960s and early '70s, Sharon McVeigh and Pippa Allen had lessons in freezing-cold Nissen huts well out of sight of the impressive Victorian hydro architecture of the main building (the part their parents saw). Sharon never passed her Maths O-level, and suffered from the sense of being 'dumped in the B stream where you did domestic science'. Only three girls did science in the sixth form and Pippa was one of them. 'They weren't geared up to teaching science,' she said. 'I got a B and a couple of Cs. They put me in to do the Oxbridge exam in the Lower Sixth and I couldn't answer a single question. I was completely out of my depth. They had no idea how to prepare me.'

I heard about countless teachers like these: story after story of under-achievement caused by unambitious teaching by bored teachers to bored girls, and the occasional harebrained scheme by a headmistress to put a girl in for some prestigious exam for which she was woefully underprepared. Then suddenly, out of wall-to-wall dreariness, a spark would come: a tiny area of a girl's education where someone managed to get some information across in an inspiring way.

These education-hungry girls have never forgotten those sparks. For example, the 1950s Southover girls were taught art by Quentin Bell, who was 'inspirational'. 'I was so bad at games,' said Cecilia Neal, 'that the games mistress almost begged me not to play. So I had extra art with another girl, and we cycled to Charleston for potting lessons with Quentin. His teaching was excellent and it was all a revelation to me.'

The Hanford girls were taught art appreciation or 'Art Apree' by the headmistress, Mrs Canning, and since then have always been able to tell a Veronese from a Titian. At Beaufront, Georgina Hammick had (for a short time) the wonderful English teacher Miss De Butts. When Georgina was 10, Miss De Butts wrote in her report, 'Unusually mature in outlook and powers of expression for her age. She uses an original and vivacious style.' And in her next report: 'An excellent examination paper showing real appreciation and wide knowledge.' 'We had to learn any poem we liked and I learned "The Battle of Naseby" and recited it,' Georgina said. 'Miss De Butts really made you try hard and made you want to do well. But then she left, after my second term.'

Her replacement was deadly dull. She wrote one-word reports: 'Good.' The loss of a good teacher is a kind of bereavement for a child. Georgina had to survive for four more years in the negative environment of Beaufront without that morale-boosting prop. But surprisingly enough, the horrible Miss Creed – she of the billowing cardigans, the punishing notices and the squeaking shoes – turned out to be an excellent (though not a nice) English and Scripture teacher. No girl who was taught a Shakespeare play by her has forgotten it, and many still know whole plays by heart thanks to her. 'Creedie acted out the dialogue and you felt she loved the stuff,' said Amanda Vesey. She also made the girls learn lots of long poems by heart, and Amanda's word-perfect knowledge of Keats's 'La Belle Dame Sans Merci' led to a seminal split-second event in her early adulthood, for which she is still grateful.

'I was staying with my sister whose husband was being rather patronizing, telling me to "pass the crumpets round" when Francis Huxley was coming to tea that afternoon, implying that I should keep quiet and know my place in this intellectual atmosphere. Well, as I was passing the crumpets round, Francis Huxley happened to be quoting "La Belle Dame" and said "... and honeydew". I quietly corrected him: "... and *manna* dew." He looked up at me, rather surprised. A few days later I received a letter from him and a wonderful love affair started ...'

As often as I heard 'the science teaching was almost non-existent' and 'I was useless at Maths' from my interviewees, I heard 'but the English teaching was very good'. Pitiful though the Bunsen-burner count was, I envied these women whose teens had not been blighted by enforced studying of the 'three-headed monster' of the sciences – Physics, Chemistry *and* Biology – each of which now has its own textbook as thick as the September issue of *Vogue* and blights the weekday evenings of countless twenty-first-century arts-minded students. In those days it was fine to concentrate on the arts if you wanted to. The timetable allowed for girls to be steeped in literature and history. They read their way through their school library, quietly widening their general knowledge.

Penny Neary remembers her English teacher at Benenden

straying off the official syllabus and introducing the class to Dylan Thomas's poetry, which inspired them all deeply. The History nun at St Mary's, Ascot charged up and down the classroom 'being' the Duke of Marlborough, bringing the Battle of Blenheim alive, and she read aloud the Duke's letters to his wife Sarah Churchill, which began 'Dearest Love'. The girls have never forgotten it. If you happened to be a naturally un-sciencey person, which many of my interviewees were, this arts-leaning state of affairs was ideal. (Sal Rivière, though, bitterly regrets the lack of science teaching at Beaufront and has made up for it in later life by devouring books on science.)

There was a headmistress at Moira House in Eastbourne in the 1940s called Mona Swann. Miss Swann's 'thing' was choral speaking – everyone speaking together, learning to attend to the physical particularity of varying sounds and to produce those sounds in 'synchrony'. She wrote a book on the subject in 1934 called *Many Voices*. This was just the kind of eccentric obsession that could work magic on certain girls. 'Mona Swann was the formative influence on Prunella Scales,' said Morar Stirling, who was there with Prunella Illingworth, as she was in those days. (Prunella's mother, whose maiden name was Scales, was a matron at Moira House during the war, when it was evacuated to the Ferry Hotel on Lake Windermere.) Miss Swann gave Prunella leading parts in the school plays, and this grounding in the musical sounds of words was seminal for her.

Mona Swann, together with the old retired headmistress

Gertrude Ingham (the daughter of the Victorian founder), who still wandered around teaching Religious Studies in the 1940s and had 'earphone hair and dressed like an Anglican nun even though she wasn't one', are an example of two spinster headmistresses who gave the girls in their charge a wonderfully rounded education in the arts and humanities that enriched their lives. 'Miss Ingham picked out the most important bits of the Bible in the King James version,' said Morar Stirling, 'and all that beautiful language has stayed with me always.'

History was well taught, with proper chronology. A 'marvellous, Mrs-Tiggy-Winkle-like old bird' called Edith Tizzard, the deputy headmistress, was a Palgrave's *Golden Treasury* fan: she made the girls learn most of the poems by heart. They did 'sonnets, odes and elegies' for their School Certificate in 1950 (the last year before the School Certificate became O-levels). With the inspirational music teacher, Taormina Mayo, the girls took part in the Bach tricentenary in 1950; were taken to the Devonshire Hall in Eastbourne to hear Yonty Solomon and Alfred Cortot; and took part in Benjamin Britten's *Let's Make an Opera*, taken up to London on a bus to sing the Little Sweep's song with Britten conducting.

Miss Swann and Miss Ingham were both utterly fascinated by the Oberammergau Passion Play and told the girls endlessly about it and showed them photographs. The school library was excellent, and on Saturday afternoons the girls read for hours, in between playing tennis and going for long walks and picnics on the Downs.

'I wouldn't say I was well-educated,' said Morar Stirling, after telling me all about that. 'I can't do fractions or decimals or speak French or Latin. But the school gave me a great sense of duty and love and care for other people, and a love of the arts and music'

Miss Swann, for all her brilliance at inspiring girls with choral speaking and Oberammergau devotion, was unambitious for her pupils. Morar remembers her saying to a girl called Louisa Service, 'I expect *you* to amount to something.' That stress on 'you' suggested that she didn't expect the vast majority of her girls to amount to much.

11

Fresh Air and Other Discomforts

I'm trying to avoid clichés, but in this chapter I will use the expression 'level playing field' in its literal sense. The grounds of Wycombe Abbey, for example, have several of these: rectangular patches of ground, formerly on a picturesque slope, but long since flattened – thanks to the games-playing vision of the school's foundress and her successors – into a suitable venue for lacrosse on every single afternoon except Sunday, in all weathers.

'Cradle!' The fierce command, shouted across the pitch on a January afternoon by a games mistress in a divided skirt, still rings in Old Girls' ears. It means: put your lacrosse stick, or 'crosse', into the air, scoop up the ball as it flies past, and run with it, swinging your stick from side to side to stop the ball falling out, before flicking it to another player in your team or into the goal. It took time to acquire this fast but delicate skill. For this reason lacrosse was ideally suited to boarding-schools, as one thing the girls did have a great deal of was time. A games mistress wrote in one of Judith Kerr's school reports from Hayes Court School in Kent in 1939, 'Judith has learned to cradle her crosse at last.' That has a Victorian-hymn-book ring about it. Oh, that we could all learn to cradle our crosse at last.

It was a fateful afternoon, for the non-gamesy members of the British girls' boarding-school population, when the first headmistress of St Leonards, Miss Lumsden, visiting Canada in 1884 for the Annual Conference of the British Association for the Advancement of Science, happened to watch a lacrosse match between the Montreal Club and the Canghuawaya Indians. She came excitedly back to Fife telling everyone about 'the new game La Crosse' and the sport was introduced to the school in the spring term, to create variety from hockey. The Big Field was levelled in 1897 and other fields followed. When Miss Dove left St Leonards to found Wycombe Abbey, she took lacrosse with her, and thus the game spread southwards. In 1902, so few schools played it that St Leonards travelled all the way to Roedean (525 miles) for an away match.

A photograph with the caption 'Girls returning from the lower hockey ground' is one of my favourites from Jane Claydon's book *St Leonards: First in the Field*. (Jane Claydon was head of PE at the school in the 1970s, and went on to become deputy head. She wrote *First in the*

Field to emphasize St Leonards' pioneering role in bringing competitive games into the world of girls' schools.)
The girls returning from the lower hockey ground in the
photograph look enchantingly happy and chatty with their
fresh, bonny faces: but is this happiness partly relief that
games are over? Would they be looking quite so happy if it
was a photograph of 'Girls on their way to the lower hockey
ground?' I know I wouldn't.

To be on your way to a games pitch is, for some, a
trudge of dread, because you know that for the next two
hours (which will pass slowly) you will be required to feign
interest in whether or not a ball goes into a goal, and will
have to be careful not to let your team down by preventing
this or helping it to go into the wrong goal. You know that
this is all supposed to foster team spirit, but your heart is
heavy with the knowledge that you will be the person who
lets your team down, because you don't care deeply enough
about where the ball goes. You will be cold, bored and
diminishing in popularity with every failed lunge.

Surprisingly enough, it has been hard for me to find a St
Leonards Old Girl who didn't enjoy hockey and lacrosse.
Thank goodness, in a way, because there was no getting
out of them, except on the first three days when you had
'the curse' (see my later chapter on 'how babies come'). I
did ask Jane Claydon what it must have been like for girls
who didn't enjoy games and she said, frankly, 'That would
be unfortunate.' Because the sandy soil of St Andrews was
well-drained, the pitches were hardly ever waterlogged

(waterlogged pitches are the games-detester's only hope). If, as sometimes happened, they were too icy to play on, the girls played hockey on the West Sands instead, or were sent on a brisk run to the third roundabout on the St Andrews links.

Mary James, who was at the school in the 1950s, remembers getting such a stitch doing this, and going so puce in the face, that she thought she was about to die. The staff were obsessed with their girls getting fresh air and exercise. Vicky Peterkin wasn't even let off cricket when her leg was in plaster. She still had to hobble to the nets for batting practice. But all the girls wanted *their* house to win 'The Shield' – the house trophy – and this rivalry, far more than rivalry with other schools, was the driving force that fired everyone's enthusiasm on freezing afternoons. 'Playing games,' Jane Claydon said to me, 'taught the girls how to lose gracefully, and how to persevere, and be dignified if things went wrong, and put up with the odd injury and generally not make a fuss.'

St Leonards, Wycombe Abbey, Roedean, Cheltenham, Sherborne School for Girls and Malvern Girls' College were institutions that modelled themselves on boys' public schools: hence the cricket. Cricket is also ideally suited to boarding-school life because it goes on for hours and soaks up whole afternoons. As Gillian Avery writes about these so-called 'girls' public schools' in *The Best Type of Girl*, 'This new breed of young woman, reared on fresh air, plain food, boys' games and cold baths, would become robust, of tireless energy, public-spirited and responsible.' To foster vigorously competitive outdoor team games seemed 'deliciously revolutionary' to the foundresses of these schools: it was a reaction against the 'drooping femininity' that the earlier, more fey female establishments had encouraged. The exciting concept of two obligatory hours per day of team games was built into the timetable. Here is Miss Flint on Miss Dove's high moral thoughts about the virtues of games:

> Sport would develop powers of organization, of good temper under trying circumstances, courage and determination to play up and do your best even in a losing game, rapidity in thought and action, judgement and self-reliance, and above all things, unselfishness.

What hope did a girl who happened to have no interest in balls going into goals have against these almost fanatical theories about the character-forming virtues of team games, and their vital importance for making a girl into a valuable member of society?

Some parents were not keen on their daughters coming home with thick calf-muscles or broken noses from too much running and stick-work, fearing that these would reduce their daughters' eligibility, and so decided against sending them to these gamesy schools. The cricket coach at Roedean in the 1950s was a formidable woman called

Cecilia Robinson, known as 'Bobbie' Robinson, vice-captain of the England women's cricket team and sister of Bishop John Robinson, who wrote the controversial book *Honest to God*. 'She would have made a wonderful *man*,' said Caroline Bingham when I asked her to describe what Bobbie Robinson looked like. Acquiring such masculine, weather-beaten looks was exactly what some of the more old-fashioned parents wanted to shield their daughters from.

Would you prefer to be sent to bracing St Leonards, with raging sea on three sides of the town, where the team spirit (according to a Wycombe Abbey girl sent there to convalesce) 'became frozen in that northern clime to a chill, intense religion'; or to Cheltenham, with its vast games pitches a full fifteen minutes' walk from the College, its daunting hierarchy of sporting kudos, and the likelihood that you would have to 'tag' as you walked there; or to Wycombe Abbey, with its two hours of games per day and extra practice before lessons for those in teams; or to Roedean, in another climate entirely from St Leonards, although you might not know it because, high up on a cliff above Brighton, the wind was so powerful that it knocked you over and threw great skeins of seaweed into the air which then flopped into the goal mouth? These are pleasurable alternatives to contemplate as an adult, tucked up in bed on a windy evening. But hundreds – thousands – of girls really did have to live those existences. 'Did you still have to play if it was pouring with rain?' I asked Cicely Taylor. To which the reply was, 'Of course! What a question!'

Here is Josephine Boyle's description of lacrosse at St Helen's, Northwood in the 1950s:

I continued to be uncoordinated, and I hated the afternoons in winter when we played lacrosse on a cold and muddy field, with hard leather balls hurtling around alarmingly near nose and teeth. You were supposed to cradle the ball within a curious contraption strung with catgut on the end of a stick, and run at the same time, half-turning this weapon rhythmically from side to side, to prevent the ball dropping out, as you ran. I could as easily have learned to fly a helicopter.

And here is Caroline Bingham on lacrosse at Roedean in the same decade:

I was very happy at Roedean, but it was ruined by games for me. We had to play lacrosse five days a week, up on the pitches overlooking the sea, battered by the wind and rain. I was wet, cold and bored, chasing a ball around that I didn't want anyway. I did get chilblains, and once you have them you have them for ever.

One of the unappealing things about lacrosse, Liz Forgan said (she played much too much of it at Benenden, also in the 1950s, lashed by the wind high up on the Weald of Kent), was that you had to grease the leather mesh of your lacrosse stick with 'horrible orange jelly from a big tub: it looked like Turkish delight'. Armed with this grease-smeared stick you then had to go out and play for hours, 'and it just seemed that you had to run and run without stopping'. Even the white lines at the edge of the pitch were not the limit, she said: 'Because lacrosse had been invented in the prairies, where there was infinite space, the rules allowed you to *run off* the pitch, far beyond the white lines.'

As Michaela Reid (pillar of the lacrosse team at Wycombe Abbey in the late 1940s) admitted to me, life at boarding-schools was *so* much easier if you enjoyed games. You were so immersed in the match, for the honour of your house or the pride of the school, that you forgot about the chilblains. The almost balletic skill of cradling your crosse could be addictive for those who loved it. Straight after lunch, these girls rushed out of doors, keen not to miss a minute.

I did speak to two early-1960s Roedean games-detesters. Caroline Bingham pretended to have 'the curse' for two whole weeks at a time in order to be let off. This worked until the matron threatened to send her to the doctor for a check-up. Rita Skinner managed to find a pink pen identical to the one her housemistress Miss Ratcliffe ('the Rat') used for signing off-games notes. 'I learned to forge her initials, "G. M. S. R.", and I did that for myself and for a few other girls.'

Anne Heseltine at St Helen's, Northwood used to hide in the Wellington-boot room to avoid games, 'until they locked it. I can remember the smell of wet rubber. Games were all-important at St Helen's – the "successful" girls were the ones who were good at games – but games were of no interest to me. I *never* wanted to be in teams.' These girls would have loved to be allowed to go for long, uncompetitive country walks instead – but this would never have been allowed: far too gentle, as well as out-of-bounds.

As soon as the summer term arrived, games became far nicer. First of all there was the delightful change to the timetable which still persists at boarding-schools: lessons straight after lunch and games afterwards, going on till supper-time on balmy evenings. Then, the games themselves were less ferocious. The gentle 'plock' of tennis balls, and the distant sound of girls calling "Vantage!" and 'Game!' is one of the romantic glories of girls' schools celebrated in Angela Brazil's novels. There were only about two days a year, the Roedean girls told me, when the wind wasn't blowing fiercely up on that cliff; but still, fielding out in the deep on a June afternoon, making daisy-chains between overs, was blissful, remembers Fi Breeze (her name matched her memory): 'We had a huge view of the sea, a wonderfully clear view, and the sound of the seagulls, and Radio Caroline sailed past.' (Radio Caroline started in 1964, so this must have been in Fi's final year.) 'Walkers came past on the cliff path and gazed at the unusual sight of girls playing cricket.'

But in the summer term there was also the outdoor swimming-pool to worry about. From April onwards girls would be made to jump into these leaf-covered expanses of water, either unheated or just about heated up to 50 degrees, causing their breathing almost to stop, such was the shock. Neither Anne Heseltine at St Helen's nor Gillian Darley at Benenden was ever actually taught to swim: Anne just splashed about in the shallow end but Gillian was told to jump into the deep end. 'I went down, twice. I remember thinking, "Maybe this is *it*."'

At Penrhos College the girls who couldn't swim had to do piggy-back races in the shallow end. The St Leonards pool was one of those natural swimming-pools that fills with seawater at high tide: just as cold as the sea but with none of the anaesthetic effect produced by waves. To get into it you had to slither down the seaweedy edge. The St Elphin's, Darley Dale girls had to swim in the unheated Matlock Hydro and it put them off swimming for life.

The evacuated Queen Margaret's, York girls at Castle Howard were made to go for swims in the vast circular Atlas fountain in front of the house, 'with Atlas in the middle holding up a bronze globe, and four tritons pouring water out of their trumpets, which rebounded off the globe on to us', said Angela Mackenzie. 'It was slimy, with frog-spawn and frogs, and you skidded on the slippery bottom if you tried to walk. You were supposed to swim round and round if you could. I never learned to swim and I still can't.' (Angela also still has a bump on her nose from a lacrosse injury sustained at Castle Howard.)

*

The 1950s and early 1960s Southover girls I spoke to were terrified of having to play matches against Roedean as Roedean girls were much more fierce and well-trained. These extracts from the Southover 1962 school magazine give a flavour of the Southover girls' unambitious attitude when it came to games:

With the help of Miss Swaine, the standard of stick work and team play improved during the term, but not sufficiently to enable the team to win any matches.

And (about netball):

The general standard of play in this game was fairly satisfactory as it does not require such a great amount of basic skill and training in the early stages. However, bad habits of footwork and passing had been developed and these showed some improvement during the year. Even so, the standard throughout the School is not sufficiently high and will only be improved by a fuller co-operation of all girls in every games lesson.

Every morning, whatever the weather, the Southover girls had to run the 'Quarter Mile', down the drive and back again – but this doesn't sound as demanding as running to the third roundabout on the St Andrews links.

At St Felix, Southwold the older girls had to take the

younger ones for walks in crocodiles round the perimeter of the grounds: once round was known as 'ones bounds'; twice was 'twos bounds'. Again, a civilized, gentle pursuit – although St Felix was quite serious about games: Tanya Harrod was athletics captain, which involved embroidering badges with an 'A' to give to the girls who were dedicated. At Oxenford Castle in the 1950s the girls had to run halfway down the South Drive and back again every morning except Sunday. (Only halfway down, mind.) Oxenford's ladylike approach to outdoorsiness is exemplified by this description of a Girl Guides expedition in the 1950s, given to me by Gillian Charlton Meyrick:

Lady Marjorie Dalrymple [who ran Oxenford with her sister Lady Eglington] was very keen on girl-guiding – she had started the Girl Guides in Borneo and New Zealand. She taught us the whistle signs and how to do knots and how to put up a tent. Only once, a group of four of us went on a local Girl Guides camp, in the Pentland Hills: a camp attended by all the girl guides from the local mining communities. *They* all took buses to the nearest village and then walked the rest of the way to the camp, carrying their tents and luggage on their backs. *We* arrived at the camp in a Rolls Royce, with Hogg, the chauffeur.

Oxenford girls did a bit of archery on the lawn, and a spot of lacrosse and tennis, and they skated on the dried-up lake in winter and grew vegetables in their own individual gardens – another of Lady Marjorie's pet enthusiasms. The headmistresses believed in fresh air but weren't obsessed with competitive games. The danger was that if you did happen to be exceedingly good at games at any of these more relaxed schools, you were not pushed to reach your full potential or to play for your county.

I had to ask, 'What are chilblains, exactly?' when I started interviewing for this book, so sheltered had I been through a radiator-warmed childhood. One Old Girl (as I have said) simply put up a crooked red finger and said 'these'. 'My mother went to a girls' boarding-school,' said another woman I met at a drinks party. 'Her toes have *never* recovered.' Angela Mackenzie told me she even got chilblains behind her ears at Castle Howard. 'It has made me frightened of the cold.' I Googled 'chilblains' and saw horrid photographs of them: red, swollen blotches on the toes and fingers. The awful thing was that when you did manage to get to a hot pipe or a fire to warm these suffering extremities, the chilblains started to itch and you were meant not to scratch them. Every single toe and finger had to be bandaged up.

Girls were also told that sitting on radiators would give them piles. But how could they resist, when warmth was strictly rationed and they were frozen to the bone after lengthy spells on the pitches or in the knife-cold water? When I interviewed my group of 1950s West Heath Old

Girls, Aurea Carter showed me her crooked fingers from the chilblains, and Phoebe Berens told me she had been sitting on a radiator (risking piles) when the news came that King George VI had died.

'You must remember,' some of these girls said to me, 'that our family houses weren't very warm either.' These girls were used to the cold: used to plunging their feet down into an ice-cold bed that never seemed to warm up. Vanessa Kent told me that Roedean in the early 1960s was actually warmer than home – at least, it was if you were inside the building.

The indoor cold was quite something. At Leelands in Kent, the prep-school run by 'Belly' and 'Tay' and a place that Liz Forgan actually loved, a hot-water pipe ten inches in diameter ran all the way along the walls of the ground floor, from room to room. That was it, as far as heating was concerned. The dormitories were unheated and the windows were kept open at night. This was absolutely typical. At Downham in Norfolk, each girl was given an exotically French-named 'carafe' of water for drinking and tooth-brushing. On winter mornings there was a thick layer of ice on top of the water in the carafe.

It's hard for us to envisage just how cold a room has to be for that to happen – and for a hot-water bottle to freeze. Face-flannels in the mornings were as stiff as boards. Both getting into bed at bedtime, and getting out again in the morning for the strip-wash, were moments to dread. At Longstowe Hall near Cambridge, during the war, you had to use the water inside your hot-water bottle to wash with in the morning: this was hard to do if the water was frozen solid. Girls had to be inventive, supplementing their bedding by tucking in pages of old newspaper to stop the gaps. At Penrhos College, after the matron had opened both windows of the dormitory for the night, creating a draught, Morag Bushell remembers stuffing the gaps with loo paper – and that was as late as the mid-1970s.

The loo paper was hard: Izal 'Medicated'. It was either that, or Jeyes 'Super Strong'. To the girls who had to use this stuff it was not the medicatedness of loo paper or the strength of it that mattered, but its absorbency, and one thing hard loo paper did not do was absorb. The true measure of a school's meanness was whether it had soft lavatory paper in the bathrooms on the 'family' side of the house (and in the one for visiting parents), and gave the hard stuff to the girls.

The iron-framed beds had lumpy mattresses, and they dipped terribly. 'Some of the parents complained, including mine,' said Josephine Boyle, remembering the dipping beds at St Helen's, Northwood in the late 1940s, 'but all the school did was to move the worst of the beds around, to allay the most recent complaints.' New beds were not easy to come by immediately after the war. 'In the summer of my first year,' Josephine said, 'London hosted the Olympic Games, and visiting teams were lodged in various boarding-schools round London. The Dutch team, including the athletics Gold Medal winner [of women's running races] Fanny Blankers-Koen, were lodged in the St Helen's dormitories. I've often wondered what they thought of our beds.'

So days, and nights, were a long catalogue of discomforts. You got out of your lumpy, dipping bed and washed your face in icy water with a frozen face-flannel, went to the loo and used 'tracing-paper loo paper' (as one of the Hanford girls vividly described it), put on your itchy, unflattering uniform, went down to an unappetizing breakfast (see my later chapter on food), went out to play a quick voluntary game of lacrosse before lessons, did your assigned task of unpaid dusting or polishing, had interminable lessons in draughty classrooms and rushed back to the house for lunch, trying to reach the common room first so you could have a brief moment sitting on the radiator.

Straight after lunch you were sent out of doors to play games for two hours, then had more lessons, then supper and prep, and then (but only if it was one of your three bath nights per week) you were allowed a quick four-inch-deep bath. A line was drawn on the inside of the baths to enforce the high-water mark. Either the school was short of hot water, in which case the younger girls were encouraged to have baths together; or the school was paranoid about lesbianism, in which case the girls were forbidden to have baths together. Then, tired out, you edged your feet down into the cold, dipping bed again and woke up the next morning with backache.

In order to make time pass in this environment till the longed-for end of term, was it preferable to have too much to do, or not quite enough? What went on in the untimetabled hours?

12

Girls Unsupervised

If you run a girls' boarding-school, do you try to keep the girls frenetically busy – with bells clanging in their ears every forty minutes to announce the start of a new enforced activity – so they don't have time to mooch about and get homesick or nasty; or do you give them hours of free time to roam around the grounds, developing their friendships and enmities, reading their way through Georgette Heyer and playing jokes on each other? Headmistresses took different approaches to the question of free time.

A Roedean Old Girl remembers life at the school being a constant race with time and being bullied by bells. Weekends were stuffed full with games, church services, prep, communal walks, clothes-mending and letter-writing. At Benenden in the late 1950s, Penny Neary spent weekend afternoons happily absorbed in her Hobby with a capital 'H': she made the whole Antarctic out of polystyrene, and this creation won points for her house. (Those competitive Benenden Hobbies, so loathed by Gillian Darley, appealed to some girls, who relished the challenge of creating a work of art to be judged.)

On Tuesday evenings Penny did bell-ringing in the village church, which she loved; she went for long walks round Benenden's lake, drawing strength from its beauty, and she took part in plays and music and went to church twice on Sundays, so there was little time for mooching about.

The 1970s St Mary's, Wantage girls I spoke to, on the other hand, said that apart from one boring chapel service there was nothing arranged for them to do in the evenings or at weekends. There were miles and miles of empty noticeboards with nothing on them except dots where drawing-pins had once been. An empty noticeboard is somehow worse than a blank wall: like a tap that doesn't give out water, or an escalator that isn't moving, an empty noticeboard shouts about what it's supposed to be doing, making you all the more aware that it is failing. About once a term a single fluttering bit of paper would be pinned up, announcing a forthcoming bus trip to Oxford for shopping. The girls, in their sack-like uniforms, flocked to this notice and there was a flurry of excitement.

Free time can bring out the best and the worst in people – and perhaps especially in girls, who can change in an instant from being the best of friends to the worst of friends, and especially in enclosed institutions, which tend to magnify whatever characteristics the inmates have. The frenetic bell-ringing schools were afraid of that 'worst': hence the packed timetable, aiming to tire girls out so they had no time for idleness, horridness or mischief. In the vast vacuum of free time at Wantage, the girls sat on radiators, chatting and planning subversive things to do.

Those long hours were the sediment that became the rock of their lifelong deep friendships. They discussed endlessly, and disparagingly, the traits of every member of staff, such as the housemistress with pale-pink eyelashes, whom they named 'Piggy Malone', the hopeless maths teacher, the awful games mistress who made them change out of their games clothes in the staffroom with the teachers watching, and the school doctor, whom they named 'Dirty Doctor Dick' – 'even though', as Georgina Petty said, 'he was perfectly normal: poor him, actually'. These characters provided limitless material and they are still talking about them forty years later.

With too much time on their hands, and a taste for thrills, the Wantage girls became fascinated by Ouija boards. In the empty hours of Saturday afternoons they sat in a circle trying to contact the restless dead who needed to pass on messages to the living. 'We contacted a spirit called John Noakes,' Georgina Petty said. 'He wanted us to give a message to his wife that he still loved her.'

The girls got into a fever of excitement about John

Noakes, desperate to help him pass the message on. They slipped out to the nearest telephone box, found 'Noakes, J.' in the local directory and rang the number. Mrs Noakes answered, and one of the girls said to her, 'Mrs Noakes? Are you on your own? We've got some news for you. We've just had a message from your husband.' Then they heard Mrs Noakes saying, 'John – there's someone on the phone for you! Sorry, love, he's in the front room watching the Grand National.'

Nothing in the girls' lives since has matched that for hilarity. The thrilling spookiness of the seance; the reckless telephone call to a total stranger; the anticlimax of Mr Noakes's alive and television-watching presence; the slight non-sequitur of Mrs Noakes's underwhelmed reaction: these were seminal moments for the girls. One can't help thinking that the fingers being mysteriously pulled from letter to letter across the Ouija board were subconsciously being encouraged to spell out the name of a *Blue Peter* presenter.

'I sometimes speak about the *dry rot* of slackness,' Miss Alice Baird wrote in her Letter to New Members of the Sixth at St James's, West Malvern in the 1930s. 'I want *you* to do your best to attack it, in whatever form it appears.' And 'In general, set an example of keenness and enthusiasm at work, games and all the other activities, so that years ahead, talking of this Sixth, the feeling one will have is *not* "They were rather a slack lot in the Sixth at that time", but "That was a splendid Sixth, they are bound to do well and be the best sort in after life."'

That gutsy, Margaret Rutherford tone of voice brings back the keenness, busyness, uprightness and purposeful-ness of those pre-war schooldays. Girls in the 1930s were not loafing around trying to contact the dead in their free time. They were sewing, tending their individual gardens, writing poems, practising the piano and playing good-mannered tennis for the honour of the school. By the 1970s, at swathes of country boarding-schools, a certain slackness had taken over – not only among the girls but also among the staff. Demoralized and exhausted after a week of unre-warding teaching from the same old antiquated textbooks, the staff shut the door on their charges and left them to themselves, except perhaps for a showing of *Genevieve* on Sunday evening.

You would think that in an establishment where the staff were either coldly uninterested in their pupils or actively nasty, this might have a trickle-down effect, making the girls correspondingly cold and nasty to each other during the long unsupervised weekend afternoons. That was going to be my theme for this chapter: that meanness at the top of a school trickled down to meanness among the girls and vice versa. But this was not necessarily the case. At St Mary's, Wantage in the 1970s, just after most of the nuns had left and the school was taken over by a succession of 'hopeless old women with grey hair' who had no idea how to run a school, showed no love towards the girls and left them with nothing to do for hours on end, the opposite happened: the girls were in fact lovely to each other.

Their method for surviving the experience was to stick together and make their own kindness and their own fun. If they happened to be caught up to no good by the house-mistress Miss Emily, who had her hair done each Thursday so it looked like 'a vast steel helmet', she shouted at them and the punishment was to go to the 'Bulge' by the chapel and stick all the broken hymnbooks back together with lick-it-yourself Sellotape.

The tired, bored staff of unmarried women at such schools could just about keep things going during the week, but at the weekend they gave up, leaving the girls with nothing to do. Westonbirt had the most beautiful grounds with grottoes, Italian gardens, and trees to climb, 'but', remembers Griselda Hailing, 'by the age of 14 or 15 you'd *done* all that. You really didn't want to go out and climb trees all afternoon. It was a four-mile walk to the nearest shop. Boredom was really the essence of our existence. I actually resorted to reading novels by Solzhenitsyn and Henry James: you have to be *very* bored to read Henry James, in my opinion.'

On Sunday afternoons there might be an occasional lecture by a visiting speaker, but these were painfully unsuited to the girls who were made to go. 'One lecture,' said Griselda, 'was by an old woman telling us how awful it was to be deaf, and how going deaf was worse than going blind. Another was on town planning. The lecturer was sneezing and coughing – basically, he had 'flu – and he droned on for *an hour and a half* about how they made the roundabouts in Brighton.' Boredom, during that lecture, became a tangible presence in the room.

Even at the more academically ambitious and better-run schools, there were countless empty hours in the 1960s and '70s. 'Please send me something to *do* at weekends,' Bridget Howard wrote in a letter to her parents from St Mary's, Ascot. 'I loved the lessons, but life outside lessons was terribly boring,' she said. 'We hung around in groups, chatting.' At weekends there were roll-calls once an hour, just to keep tabs on everyone. The 16-year-olds had their own common room – but there was nothing in it, apart from some chairs and a gramophone. They would have loved a kettle, or a toaster, but those were forbidden. Only the prefects were ever allowed to make toast, in a little room upstairs, on Sunday afternoons, out of a few slices of bread sent up by a nun.

That weekly toast-making was the only perk of being a prefect. We forget, nowadays, the scarcity of treats that made a piece of self-made toast extraordinarily exciting: something you would spend your whole teens striving towards. In an enclosed and rule-ridden world, with little access to money or shops, tiny treats became important. 'All your friends gave you holy cards on saints' days,' Mary Miers said. 'We loved having *stuff* to look at in our missals.' If you were given a bath-cube by a friend in your dormitory for your birthday, or a pack of Waverley Notelets, this was an event worth writing home about.

A lot of fainting went on, both real and fake. 'Fake' fainting was when you rocked someone back and forth and then suddenly squeezed them hard in the waist, causing them to keel over. This was a common pastime for weekend afternoons. Real fainting happened at St Felix, Southwold, Tanya Harrod said, mainly in the Lent term, because that was the term with no half-term, so you didn't go home for two months, and this sense of being stuck at school without end would cause odd behaviour such as fainting to break out. Sometimes odd behaviour at boarding-schools was a cry for help. A girl would suddenly and clandestinely start doing something odd and unsavoury, such as wiping her bottom on her bath towel rather than with loo paper, or leaving blood-stained sanitary towels in full view on the windowsill. This kind of thing was a hazard of too much imprisoned free time.

Girls played jacks for hours on end. We worry now that our children are literally 'left to their own devices' – i.e. electronic devices – at weekends, but was the game of jacks so much more educative? Jacks involved throwing a tiny ball up into the air and swiftly picking up a small three-dimensional x-shaped piece of metal alloy, letting the ball bounce only once, and then catching it. Then you had to do the same picking up two jacks, then three, then four and so on up to ten. Ten was very difficult.

As I remarked in the first paragraph of this book, girls with time on their hands also became experts at cat's cradle: this pointless pastime involved putting a circle of string round each hand twelve inches apart, and intertwining fingers and string in such a way as to make shapes that didn't really look much like either the Eiffel Tower or the Devil's Fork.

Girls sent off for free items and then waited impatiently for the postman's van. They wrote to the headquarters of Mars in Slough, complaining that they'd had a faulty Mars Bar, hoping to be sent a whole box of them as compensation, which sometimes happened, but the box was confiscated.

They went on strike. At Heathfield in the 1970s Bolla Denehy's whole year went on strike – though they could hardly claim to be living in conditions of overwork. 'We wrote a ridiculous letter to the headmistress, making demands,' Bolla said. 'Then we walked out of the school and sat in a forest all day long, bored and freezing cold. When we tried to go back, we found they'd locked all the doors and windows and pinned all the curtains together with the coloured bows they normally gave us for being good. One girl punched a window and broke it. We had to go and see the headmistress, who was crying. She said, "I'm going to expel you all." And we said, "If you do, how will you afford your fur coats?" She didn't expel us. Our parents all got letters. That was a case of appalling behaviour.'

Unsupervised girls listed silly names of books in the backs of their diaries: *Rusty Bedsprings* by I. P. Nightly, *Dentistry* by Phil McCavity, *Race to the Loo* by Will E. Make It, and so on – that was the height of schoolgirl humour. Diary-keeping itself was another absorbing activity: recording the saga of weekly hair-washes, other girls' birthdays, and what was for supper. Mary Miers made a point of filling the whole page of her diary for every single day, even if there wasn't quite enough to say. So, reading it, we live the long, slow hours when her trunk is packed, in proper layers with the 'function dress' laid out on top, the classrooms and dormitories are dusted and cleaned, Mother Bridget has given her two utterly predictable bits of advice for the holidays ('Be helpful at home' and 'Remember Mass on Sundays and Holy Days of Obligation'), and her parents still haven't arrived to take her home.

As well as writing those imagined book titles in the backs of their diaries, girls wrote lists of the real books they had read, and these lists are impressive. Sophia Ruck at St Mary's, Ascot read twenty-nine novels in the summer term of 1976, by (among others) Rumer Godden, Monica Dickens, Daphne du Maurier and Hester Burton (seven of her historical novels). That was typical. In those long, untimetabled hours girls found time to read, and thus they learned how to spell, when to use semicolons, and what it must have been like to be Mary, Queen of Scots.

They were attracted rather than daunted by thick novels, which were a sop to boredom. Victoria Mather at Woldingham sat on the stairs and started *Tess of the D'Urbervilles* one afternoon and didn't get up until she'd finished the whole book. At Badminton in the 1960s there was an Agatha Christie craze: starting with the then-titled *Ten Little Niggers,* Christie's novels were passed round from one girl to another ('I'm next!' 'You're not!') and read under the bedclothes by torchlight. Ann Barnes at St Mary's, Wantage in the 1940s read and read: 'I read books under the table in lessons, and during prep-time, and that was my education, really.'

No one knew what went on behind the closed doors of girls' boarding-schools in the evenings and at weekends, and many people who should have cared didn't. In 1971 a sociologist called Mallory Wober decided to find out. He visited twenty-three of them (unnamed, although we know one of them was St Felix, Southwold because Tanya Harrod remembers him as an inspirational presence) and took polls from the girls and the staff which he published in a book, *English Girls' Boarding Schools.* What were the girls like to each other when the staff weren't looking?

Here is a sample of the girls' nicknames Wober came across while he was investigating: Baggy, Bambam, Bouncy, Bubbles, Bunny, Doodles, Farto, Flea, Hairy, Kipper, Maxie, Moo, Paw-Paw, Pussy, Tick, Turnip and Wopsy. And here is a sample of the things these girls anonymously said about each other:

> Girls who tell tales are called splits . . . they are not spoken to and apple-pie beds are made, sometimes the mattress is put in the cupboard and their beds made on the springs.

[If a girl told tales] I would hit her head on a tree trunk and make her cry and send her to Coventry. I would call her a bloody little bastard (maybe bitch) – excuse the language – then ignore her completely – maybe give her a cold stare now and then.

One girl has no friends and most unluckily is on our table and she always starts arguments by kicking people. We always groan when she has more food because she is so greedy and she cries at least five times a day.

Those quotes chill the blood of anyone who remembers being bullied or unpopular at their girls' boarding-school, or anyone who remembers the unpopular girl who hung around on her own in the boot-room in abject misery, because to be seen with her was social death. The quotes plunge us straight into the very worst of girls unsupervised. They remind us of the subtle but terrifying ganging up that girls can do – 'we' being annoyed by 'her' and deciding to make her life a misery. The third quote reminds us that the very state of being unhappy ('she cries five times a day') is itself a recipe for unpopularity. What is most despised is 'wetness' and 'weediness', and crying is a symptom of those. So an unhappy girl could be locked into a vicious circle of misery and unpopularity and could not tell any grown-up, because the crime of all crimes was to be a telltale.

*

Among the stories I've been told, three particular instances of girls being vile to each other stand out. I will recount them here.

At Downe House in the early 1950s the classroom called 4B was 'the divorce classroom'. It had doors on each side, which made it ideal for the purpose. When a clique decided they didn't want to be friends with you any more there was a formal divorce process, and it took place in 4B. The 13-year-old Amanda Theunissen was formally divorced in this way. 'I suddenly found that the other girls weren't laughing at my jokes any more. That was the warning sign. This was how the divorce process worked: you were called down to 4B. As you came in through one door, all the girls who *had* been your friends walked out through the other. That was it. From that moment on you were an outcast. You were allowed to go around with the one disabled girl and the two foreigners who weren't princesses.'

Amanda has never felt as utterly unprotected as she did at that moment. There was no one to appeal to. The story makes us weep, not only for Amanda but also for the disabled girl – 'she had something wrong with her arm, and greasy hair, and wore thick round glasses', Amanda said – and for the non-royal foreign girls, who had never even been invited into a clique. Their loneliness and homesickness can only be imagined.

Is it worse to have been included and then sacked than never to have been included at all? These are questions Amanda still ponders. 'I hated Downe House with a total passion,' she told me. There was a trickle-down effect of snobbishness: the headmistress's remark about her mother running a café was echoed in the girls' snobbish attitudes towards each other, and the girls who flounced out of 4B on that fateful afternoon were the kind whose families did open their houses to the public.

At Beaufront in the 1950s, the horridness of Miss Richards and Miss Creed bred an air of mistrust in the school. A fountain pen would go missing and everyone would suspect everyone else and the whole school would be kept in for days till the culprit owned up. Georgina Hammick wrote a 'ridgy' – an 'original' piece of writing – for another girl, who asked her to, and it won the prize, and the other girl went up to collect it and didn't give Georgina as much as a tiny wink of gratitude. But that wasn't the worst story. Georgina has a more haunting memory:

We were meant to wear cream Viyella shirts, but my sister and I had poplin ones, and they were white, not cream, because our mother thought they were nicer. We *longed* for cream Viyella ones. Eventually we grew out of the shirts, and our mother at last sent us the right ones! We were thrilled. I went to my drawer to get out my lovely new shirt, and to my horror I found a shabby old Viyella shirt with broken buttons and sweat stains under the arms. It had my name tape sewn into it. I said to the housemistress, 'This is not my shirt.' To which she replied, 'You must be telling lies. It has your name on it.

Don't make such a fuss.' So I was made to wear it. It was matted, smelly and sweaty. I *knew* that someone must have swapped the shirts round and sewn my name tape into it and her name tape into mine.

Years later, when I was married and with children, I met up with a group of other mothers, and while we were swinging our toddlers on the swings and chatting about our schooldays, one of them said, 'I did something dreadful once. I had a terrible old shirt at school and I swapped it with another girl's new shirt, and changed the name tapes round.' I said, 'That was MY shirt. I went through hell because of that. So it was you!'

This story shows how long our childhood crimes linger in the conscience: the other mother was suitably horrified and embarrassed at being thus exposed in adult life.

A new girl at Badminton in 1961, Markie Robson-Scott lay in bed in her dormitory while the other girls told her about a lovely tradition at the school: 'Big Laundry'. Every week the girls sent their clothes to the laundry in a laundry bag with an accompanying list, naming the clothes in the bag. At the end of term, the girls told her, you could write the names of other items at the end of your list, such as '10 bars of chocolate' or 'a radio'. If you did that, those items would come back in the laundry bag. A radio! Markie longed for a radio more than anything. 'Is that really true?' she asked. 'Yes!' All term, she was excited about Big Laundry, and the dormitory head kept talking about it. At last the final week

of term arrived and Markie duly wrote her list of requests
at the end of her laundry list. She was all excitement. A few
days later the laundry bag came back. It was worryingly
soft and light. She felt around inside it, quaking. It only
contained clothes: no chocolates, and no radio.

'You didn't really *believe* that, did you?' the other girls
jeered.

Markie still hasn't quite got over that episode. It was the
prototype for all of life's hopes being tantalizingly raised
and then brutally dashed. She had arrived at Badminton
an easygoing and trusting girl after happy years at Miss
Ironside's in London. She had been tremendously excited
about going to boarding-school, having read *Malory Towers*.
But 'everyone was cruel and mean. In those first school
holidays I didn't speak to my parents at all. I just practised
jacks. I got very good at it and I also got good at being
mean. I thought, "I'm going back next term and I'm going
to be mean, like everyone else." And I was.'

Those are my three prime examples of the cruelty of girls
and its sometimes contagious effect; but there were many
more. Girls at the receiving end had to decide what to do:
either to become just as mean as everyone else, or to become
introverted or freakily religious. One Wycombe Abbey Old
Girl I spoke to, who was there in the 1970s and asked to
remain anonymous, resorted to self-harm: 'I would just play
the piano for hours on end, and I'd whack my fingers really
hard on the keyboard if I didn't get it right. I just hid away,

feeling terrible about myself.' Every term, she said, someone had to be bullied. 'How come it's my turn this term?' she remembers asking, and one of her 'friends' (now enemies) replied, 'I don't know why – we're just all being horrid to you.' She did become a religious freak and also a swot: she and another girl broke into one of the classrooms at 4 a.m. to revise.

It would have been unthinkable for this girl at Wycombe Abbey, or for Markie at Badminton, to go to any of the staff for advice or help. Pastoral care of the kind we expect now from motherly housemistresses and kind married matrons simply wasn't there. The matron at Wycombe Abbey was 'creepy physically – small and wizened – and you wouldn't want to go to her unless you were made to'. The housemistress would only talk to you if you were 'in trouble' – that is, if you had done something wrong.

In an effort to become more popular, Markie constructed fake parents who were glamorous and travelled a lot and didn't care about her. This helped a bit, giving her a whiff of exotic neglectedness. But a sudden sense of the utter futility of life engulfed her one afternoon in the school library in the middle of term when she was 15. Badminton was a slightly less right-wing girls' school than most, and religiously open-minded: the girls were allowed to cycle to whichever church they liked on Sundays (with their 2p piece in their glove for the collection), including Quaker meetings, and they appreciated this. Some of the more politically minded girls arranged days of fasting and silence for anti-apartheid. Polly Toynbee was a pupil. 'My CND activities were much frowned on,' Polly told me; 'definitely not approved. God, how I hated that school!' She used to give her fellow pupils talks about the potential horrors of nuclear war. When the sense of utter futility engulfed Markie, therefore, she was almost paralyzed, both by the sense of the total pointlessness of life, and by the dread of civilization being wiped out by a nuclear bomb. 'It didn't occur to me to talk to a member of staff about all this,' she said. She suffered in sleepless, panic-stricken silence.

What made life survivable was dancing to records all Saturday afternoon in the science lab. That, as well as reading novels, revising for exams, and being mean (sometimes resorting to physical, scratching, hair-pulling fights) was what the Badminton girls got up to in their free time, and, as there were no boys around, they were uninhibited enough to dance their heads off and sing along with their heart and soul, as if they were performing on *Top of the Pops*.

The final 'girls unsupervised' activity I'm going to address – reserving anything to do with sex and romance for a later chapter – is that of running away. An example of this most daring of unsupervised activities happened at Sibton Park when I was there, in 1974. At bedtime one evening, three beds were empty: the beds of Georgina Gore, Joanna Ansdell and Tigga Stainton. They had gone.

Georgina was the ringleader. She was later to become

the Duchess of Norfolk. Forty years after the event I went to visit her at her house in Chelsea. What exactly had happened that night?

Her driving motive, she said, was to prove to her father that she had meant it when she had said to him, on being informed she was to go back to Sibton after being promised she could go to a day school instead, 'Well, I'll run away then.' 'My father had not taken me at all seriously when I'd told him I was going to run away, but as I said those words I had a core of utter determination to show him I meant it.'

The first thing she needed to do was to compile the running-away notebook. She enlisted two co-runners-away, Tigga and Joanna, neither of whom had her core of determination but both of whom liked the idea of the adventure and were happy to go along with it. 'Of course we had to have a notebook, which we kept hidden,' Georgina said. 'We listed what we were going to need: three camp-beds, a tent, water-bottles, food, money.' The whole enterprise seemed very much in the realms of the imagination, because how were they ever going to acquire these necessary items of equipment when no Sibton girl was even allowed to go to the village shop to buy a Milky Way?

'Then, one Sunday,' said Georgina, 'I was taken out by a friend for the day, and when I arrived back at school Tigga said to me, "Our notebook's been found. We're in dead trouble."'

Those words, 'in dead trouble', might not frighten the reader now. It's hard to recapture the feeling of shaking fear and sickening dread that kept young boarding pupils in check in those days. Remember, these girls were miles from home, with no mobile phones and no parents to appeal to. Matron, the woman who chiefly ruled the Sibton girls' lives, was genuinely as terrifying as Mrs Danvers.

'So,' Georgina continued, 'I said to the others, "Come on, then, let's go tonight." "But we haven't got our stuff!" the other two protested. But I said, "It doesn't matter: we're going *now*."'

And – with no sleeping-bags, tent, water-bottle, food or money – off the three girls went, at dusk, through the woods at the back of the school and out into the fields beyond.

'It was the best feeling in my life,' Georgina said. 'There we were, just running and running. We climbed over a stile into a cornfield and ran through it: I remember that exhilaration, that sense of total liberation. We just ran and ran and ran. At one point we saw Uncle Hew on a horse, probably out looking for us. ['Uncle Hew' was Hew Service, the son-in-law of the headmistress.] So we just hid until he was out of sight, and then we carried on running. I remember it all like a film.'

Then it grew dark. In the new and eerie darkness Joanna said, 'I don't think this is such fun after all – maybe we should go back?' Georgina had no intention of doing any such thing: 'I was dead determined: I just wanted to *go*: I didn't care where. I wanted to sleep in the wood. For me it was lovely. But Tigga suggested, "Let's go and find a house and knock on the door and ask if we can spend the night."'

Georgina's heart sank at this suggestion; but she had no choice. It was two against one. This being affluent rural East Kent, the door they knocked on happened to be a large farmhouse belonging to friends of Tigga's parents. They were surprised to see three well-brought-up panting 11-year-old schoolgirls at the front door.

'We've run away,' said the girls. 'Please can we have a bed for the night?'

'Do come in,' said the nice grown-ups. The girls stepped into the warm farmhouse and into a world of kindness, the world of friends of Tigga's parents, the world of carpets, dogs and hot chocolate in a cheerful kitchen. 'They were really good to us,' Georgina said. 'Lovely people. They said, "You really had better go back to school, you know; you won't be in trouble; everyone will understand."'

In the hall Georgina could hear the clicking sound of the telephone's dial as the man of the house telephoned the school. 'We have three of your girls here . . . '

'And very soon the school came to collect us. They were nice to us until we got into the car, and as soon as we were in they said, "You are a disgrace. You have caused mayhem."'

Which indeed they had, as Hew Service recalled when I met him to hear his side of the story. 'I remember the worry of it. The palpitations, the anxiety.'

The girls were kept in confinement in the main part of the house that night: the scented, carpeted, mahogany, pot-pourri side. Later the next day they were released back into the community but we were told we should not talk to them. With horror and fascination we watched as Joanna slowly pulled up her skirt, pulled down her white summer pants and showed us five red parallel stripes across her buttocks. All three girls had been caned.

The girls' parents had been asked to choose whether their daughters should be caned or expelled. Being expelled in those days was an irredeemable disgrace: with a criminal record like that, their daughters would never be accepted by any other school and would probably never find a suitable husband.

Georgina certainly did find a suitable husband. When she was a young married countess, she received a friendly letter from Sibton asking whether she would be kind enough to be one of the donors to their appeal. She sent them £5.

13

'Would You Like Some Salt?'

The very same pudding – sponge-roll with red jam smeared along the surface and oozing out of both ends – was known as 'Dead Man's Leg' at Wycombe Abbey, 'Matron's Leg' at St Elphin's, Darley Dale, 'Granny's Leg' at Southover, and 'Reverend Mother's Leg' at the Presentation Convent in Matlock.

This shows how very like a varicose-veiny or actively bleeding human leg the puddings must have looked, sparking similar anatomical nicknames across the different schools. What could girls do, faced with the often revolting items of food they were given and made to finish, but lighten up the experience by giving them macabre nicknames? Often they named the lukewarm creations that came up from the kitchen after a part of a human or animal body or an effluent of, or ointment for, one of these. Stew was 'pterodactyl's hooves' or 'Stalin's remains'. Sago pudding was 'phlegm'. Pink blancmange was 'baby's bottom'. Lemon curd tart was 'Vaseline tart'. At Badminton, the word for muesli was 'Arabian muck' – which sounds like a nickname one of the more snobbish headmistresses might have given to the 'foreign girls who weren't princesses'.

'Of course, there was a war on,' said the 1940s girls I spoke to. 'Of course, there was still rationing, right up to 1954,' said the early-1950s girls. 'We were hungry all the time and didn't complain. We just got on with it.' School food in those rationed days was not supposed to be a pleasure. It was a necessity, to fill you up, warm you up, and give you the energy to get you through the next few hours. To make food delicious would have gone against the grain of these establishments. It would have encouraged sensuality, self-indulgence and fussiness.

The wartime Old Girls told me about the powdered egg which, when made into scrambled egg, came out like savoury custard. They also told me about the two-ounce pot of butter and two-ounce pot of margarine each girl was given to last a week. These were kept in a cupboard in the dining-room, making the cupboard smell rancid. 'One bullying girl at Cheltenham took my butter and gave me her marge,' said Pat Doyne-Ditmas, still outraged seventy years after the event.

Some schools requisitioned both the butter and the marge and bashed them into one large shape, to be shared out through the school for the week. You could tell, from the darker and paler yellows of the shape, which areas were butter and which were marge. At teatime it was margarine or butter one day and jam the next, and never the two together. Patricia Lombe-Taylor, who had been brought up on a farm, missed butter so much at Heathfield that on non-butter days she spread lanolin on her bread instead, just to get the greasy experience she craved.

Parents who lived on farms tried to supplement their daughters' diet. Patricia's mother sent her food parcels from the family farm: 'apples from our orchard, which I ate and then sold the cores to my friends for sixpence each. I had to make sure there was enough left on the core to make it worth the money for them.' Her mother also sent her eggs from the home hens; but rather than being allowed to eat her egg fried or boiled, Patricia was made to drink it, raw, in a glass of milk, supervised by the matron. She knew this was 'good for her' but she could hardly get the slimy concoction down, and the memory still makes her stomach heave.

When you had been out on the lacrosse pitch in the freezing cold all afternoon, and then had lessons in an unheated classroom, as well as doing your 'domestic work', you were so starving by the time you reached the dining-room that you would devour anything, from milk pudding to spam fritters. This was the theory, at least, and for some girls it was true. But others found it extremely hard and still feel sick remembering the ordeal. Some actually were sick while living it. You had to eat up. Girls at boarding prep-schools were made to sit all afternoon or evening in front of the congealing mess.

At Sibton Park, if you asked the riding mistress, Miss Lockwood, for a small helping of cauliflower cheese, she gave you an extra-large one to spite you. The only hope of *getting* a small helping was to ask her for a large one. But that brought the risk of getting a large one. Jackie Kingsley told me that her late sister Judy (who would become the Conservative MP for Newbury) could not eat fish pie without vomiting. She vomited at her prep-school (The Grange in Old Welwyn), so they let her off fish pie. When she arrived at Wycombe Abbey she told the authorities that fish pie made her sick, but she was made to eat it anyway and she vomited again, twice, in the dining-room. After that the school relented. But it took two major vomiting incidents for her to buck the system.

Floorboard cracks and jacket or skirt pockets were useful. Girls will go a long way to avoid putting something disgusting into their mouths. One method was to throw small handfuls of food on to the floor – always remembering to throw it to the left or right so it couldn't be traced to you. Rats and mice lived on gristly meat and gravy from discarded handfuls of stew that found their way through cracks. When they'd finished these they ate through the wiring.

Putting pilchards into one's pocket was a risky business: Gillian Darley at Riddlesworth Hall in Norfolk stuffed her pocket with pilchards rather than eat them, and managed to flush them down the lavatory, but her pocket stank of pilchards for a week. A cruel after-effect of pocket-stashing was that your pocket smelled for days of the very foodstuff you most loathed. Rosemary Chambers at Woldingham put her semolina into her pocket and it started to ooze out at the moment when the school gathered to say their nightly prayers beneath the *Mater Admirabilis*, the picture of the Madonna in a jewelled crown.

Friday fish was universally dreaded. Friday: the day of the crucifixion; the day of self-denial; the day of fish. Not fish and chips, but fish and mashed potato: soft, bony whiteness with soft, lumpy whiteness. All week long the pervading smell along boarding-school corridors was that of overcooked cabbage; but on Fridays it changed to the smell of fish being either deep-fried in old fat or slowly boiled in milk.

At Wycombe Abbey in the 1950s they used the same deep-frying fat to make the doughnuts for the next day, so the doughnuts tasted of fish. At St Leonards, Friday fish came in curried form, pocked with raisins, and was so disgusting that the girls who had eaten it smeared their teeth with toothpaste afterwards to smother the aftertaste. At Cheltenham in the late 1940s, Friday lunch was brown whale meat with thick white sinews running through it – 'and the knives and forks', said Jennifer McGrandle, 'still smelled of the herrings that the boarders had had for supper the previous night'.

'Skin on top' was a running theme. The skin on top of the fish pie was not fish skin but the wrinkled skin of fish-infused milk, pierced by the occasional upward-pointing fishbone. The skin on top of the pink blancmange at Heathfield in the 1940s, remembers Patricia Lombe-Taylor, 'was so thick that it was like a floor-covering'.

Centralized dining had not been invented: meals took place in the small dining-rooms of the separate boarding-houses and were cooked in the different house kitchens, usually by 'a woman from the village' who had no idea how to make the best of ingredients. If you glimpsed a Roedean house kitchen as you walked by, all you could see were great vats on the boil, remembers Rita Skinner. 'The food was vile: just one up from prison slop. They employed people to cook who didn't *like* cooking and didn't *want* to cook.'

It would never have occurred to these clueless cooks to brown the onions or the meat, or to add seasoning or herbs. They just threw great armfuls of cheap bony meat, fatty mince or veiny offal into the vats, added onions and water, put it all on the hob and hoped the heat and the hours would do the rest. Caroline Cranbrook still feels ill when she remembers the 'slabs of greyish ox liver tunnelled through with huge veins' that she was forced to eat at Wings, or the 'aged mackerel, which was particularly disliked, not only because it was usually a bit "off", but also because of the widely held belief that mackerel lived off dead sailors'.

The food was stodgy. The classic sponge pudding was actually called 'stodge' and was served hot at lunchtime and cold again for supper. A typical day's menu in a girls' boarding-house at St Leonards in the 1950s would be: porridge for breakfast; iced buns and cocoa for break; meat, potatoes and cabbage for lunch followed by apple pie and custard; bread and jam for tea; and cauliflower cheese tart for supper. 'I put on two stone in my first term,' said Victoria Peterkin, who actually loved St Leonards and told me that the food there was delicious. The chef had been properly trained at a cookery school, which helped.

The iced buns came from a local bakery in St Andrews. What boarding-school girls longed for were things like that – things that couldn't be tampered with by the people in the school kitchens, whose very touch spelled ruin. At Wings, Caroline Cranbrook was kept going by the iced buns at break-time. Tripling up as servant, teacher and nanny, she laid them out, doled them out to the hungry juniors, and cleared up at the end. At Westonbirt, freezing after walking through the frosty grounds from lessons in their cloaks, the girls helped themselves to iced buns and cups of cocoa and took them down to 'Hades', the basement of the enormous Victorian pile and the whirring engine-room of its heating system. Hades, with iced buns and cocoa, was a wonderfully warm place in which to spend break-time.

Judith Kerr named the stodgy food at Hayes Court during the war as one of the reasons why the place was rather depressing to be at: 'We all got very fat. On top of all the stodgy school food, in the fifth form you were allowed to walk down to the village and buy great bags of broken biscuits from Woolworth's. As soon as girls left school their mothers would put them on a diet and they had their hair done. They were unrecognizable.'

The wartime and post-war excuse for bad food was rationing and lack of money. For reasons of economy, for example, it was considered acceptable at Cheltenham to serve up, for pudding, misshapen lumps of last week's left-over cake reincarnated and suspended in jelly. But Catherine Freeman's experience at the evacuated Assumption Convent in Herefordshire shows that rationing and lack of money were no excuse for horrible food. The lay sisters who did the cooking at the Assumption Convent (it being a French order of nuns) were French. With their innate sense that eating should be a pleasure, they managed to make the school food taste good in spite of the scarcity of butter and sugar. No overcooked cabbage here: the girls were given *purée d'épinards* made from home-grown spinach, and delicious chestnut jam made from the fruit of the hedgerows. 'A great treat on high days and holidays,' said Catherine, 'were "Assumption tarts": three-cornered pieces of flaky pastry filled with homemade jam. That was a recipe left over from the Siege of Paris.'

Boarding-school food went on being bad for two and a half decades after rationing had ended and Elizabeth David had introduced the rest of the country to flavour.

The unspoken reason was that teaching girls to eat unpalatable food was part of their training in self-denial, and would enable them to cope with whatever life might throw at them. There were two theoretical extremes of 'what life might throw at you'. One was 'finishing up in a gulag', as Jackie Kingsley put it. If you finished up in a gulag, she said, you would certainly be able to cope with the food if you'd endured the meals at The Grange in Old Welwyn during the war. The other extreme was the Buckingham Palace banquet. If you were invited to a Buckingham Palace banquet, you would manage to eat gracefully whatever was put in front of you – not that it was likely ever actually to be veiny liver, fish pie or bony stew.

So girls were trained in unfussiness. To drink down a whole mug of milk, if you loathed drinking milk, was an exercise in subduing the self. You just had to shut your eyes, do it, try not to think about it, and know that it would soon be over. The same with forcing down a whole thick edge of soft pork-chop fat or (a regular on the menu at 1950s Wycombe Abbey) a plate of stewed rabbit with all its innards floating around. For many, this training in self-abnegation made meals traumatic. What should and could have been a thrice-daily pleasure was twisted into a thrice-daily nightmare.

The idea of giving any leniency to girls who didn't like certain foodstuffs was utterly against the principles of the staff. They saw it as their moral duty to stick rigidly to the rule that everything must be eaten. The adjective 'fussy' was one of the worst that could be applied to a child in those days; and a small, harmless preference counted as fussiness.

Liz Forgan's experience at Leelands exemplifies the obsession. Being a Scot, Liz preferred her porridge with salt and without sugar. At Leelands, the porridge was (a) lumpy, and (b) already sprinkled with sugar that was seeping into it. Liz could handle the lumpiness (just), but the sugar was too much. What's more, she was rather plump in those days and did not need all that extra sugar. She asked to have her porridge without sugar. Miss Belshaw and Miss Taylor said no. Her parents wrote to plead with Belly and Tay. 'Basically, World War Three broke out,' said Liz. 'The mistresses wouldn't budge. To me this seemed like the end of the world. The worst thing was that I couldn't see the reason for it. It was possibly the cruellest thing that ever happened to me.'

Though the training in unfussiness might work for half the boarding-school population, for the other half it was counterproductive: as soon as they left, they vowed never to let any of the detested foodstuffs near their mouths again. Half a century later they still avoid certain aisles in the supermarket.

Once (but only once) a week, Leelands breakfast consisted of the most delicious thing imaginable: deep-fried bread with marmalade. All girls seemed to love fried bread, the more brittle and oil-soaked the better. Liz Forgan has tried to recreate this delicacy in later life, but has realized that in order to get the authentic experience you need a deep-fryer: the bread needs to be plunged right into the oil and deep-fried to a crisp.

You could be lucky: the woman who did the cooking could happen to be a decent cook. At Beaufront in the 1950s, surprisingly enough, where most things were pretty horrid, the cooking was good, if not particularly healthy. Mrs Todd (the 'Mrs' being honorary) had come back to Camberley from Somerset where Beaufront had been evacuated during the war, and she had a wonderful way with Sunday Yorkshire pudding, remembers Sal Rivière. 'It was thick, doughy batter smothered with the gooey juices of the roast beef. Delicious! She also made nourishing soups for our supper. Less good were her lentil rissoles that stuck to the roof of the mouth.'

Girls craved sweetness, in establishments where the apple crumble consisted of cooking apples covered in a thick layer of flour. At Southover in the 1950s, the girls were given one slice of fruit cake on Sundays; it was known as 'railway cake', being the kind of cake served in railway station cafés. If your parents paid extra, you could be one of the lucky girls who had 'extra fruit': each week a consignment would be delivered in a van, from Harrods, in a box with your name on it, all the apples individually wrapped in tissue paper and resting on a bed of straw. The other sugar fix came from the daily spoonful of Radio Malt you could queue up for at the school surgery. This glutinous substance tasted deliciously of molasses, and lots of my interviewees lived for it.

*

The school food might have been neither delicate nor exquisite, but the girls' table-manners were both. Gathered round the gristle and the slop, they behaved as if they really were at a Buckingham Palace banquet.

Never, ever, at just about all the schools I have mentioned so far, were you allowed to say, 'Please may I have some salt?' Instead, you had to say, 'Would you like some salt?' The person to whom you addressed this question was never, ever supposed to reply, 'No, thank you.' The correct reply was 'No, thank you, but would you?'

This rule meant that you spent whole mealtimes scanning the table with searchlight eyes, anticipating who might be about to need what. This was a useful distraction to take your mind off the actual food. Once you had secured the salt in this subtle manner, how did you apply it to the plate? Anne Hancock has never forgotten. In her first week at Cheltenham she was summoned to her housemistress's study. 'I was terrified. What had I done wrong? I knocked on the door and Mrs Garner said, "Come in." She looked up at me from her desk, and said, "Anne: *no* lady sprinkles her salt."'

Salt must be put into a heap on the edge of the plate, not sprinkled all over. Stew must be eaten with a knife *and* a fork, not just a fork. Soup must be retrieved from the bowl by pushing your spoon backwards rather than forwards. A slice of bread and butter should never be eaten before being cut up into quarters.

On top of all this etiquette, you might be asked to

'sit up'. Sitting up meant not only sitting with your back straight, but sitting *up* at the end of the table, next to the housemistress or another member of staff. Here, you would be expected to make polite conversation throughout lunch. Termly lists of place-settings were drawn up, so you didn't just sit with your friends but were mixed up and required to make conversation with girls of other ages and with adults. Again, this was good training for the Buckingham Palace banquet or the diplomatic dinner party. As Rita Skinner put it, 'You can always tell a Roedean girl: she can keep her end up anywhere. We can talk for Britain.'

Conversation was as much the point of mealtimes as food. Even at Hatherop in the 1970s, where academic standards were at rock-bottom and girls started leaving in droves, the new headmistress Dr Pandora Moorhead kept up Mrs Fyfe's tradition of dressing for dinner on Saturday evenings. The girls put on their long Laura Ashley dresses in sprigged-flower prints with ruffles and frills round the bottom, and processed into the gloomy castle dining-room to make conversation with each other over supper.

Midnight feasts and smuggling food into school were not just a response to gnawing hunger: they were also a vital outlet for the urge felt by inmates of rule-filled institutions to assert their independence. Bridget Howard stressed this, while describing the delicious clandestine moments of enjoying smuggled food at St Mary's, Ascot in the 1960s — a school so strict that some girls in the year above her, who had dared to smuggle in a kettle and make coffee in the attic, were almost expelled for this crime.

'It was a good idea to hide smuggled food in plain sight, if you could. So I camouflaged my tube of Nestlé milk by keeping it among the toothpaste tubes. The nuns never noticed it wasn't toothpaste. I managed to hide some packets of soup, and we stirred the powder into our tooth-mugs with hot water from the tap. Doing this was our way of surviving psychologically – of keeping our independence. We felt a million dollars after doing that. It was a ritual of feeding ourselves: we shared everything and felt triumphant that we were not just living on what *they* gave us.' At girls' boarding-schools across the country, at dead of night, girls were hacking open cans of baked beans and trying to heat them over a candle.

A whole system of contraband went on out of sight of the staff. Parents wrapped edible items up inside pocket handkerchiefs and sent them off in parcels; their daughters became good at opening the parcels in full view of the supervising mistress without revealing the contents. One of the reasons why these girls were not thinking about sex all the time was because they were fantasizing about food instead. But were they thinking about sex at all?

14

Romance, Pashes and How Babies Come

'Did you have sexual thoughts, while you were a teenager at Beaufront in the late 1940s?' I asked Sal Rivière, as we sipped tea in her Wiltshire kitchen.

'Not sexual thoughts, so much as *romantic* thoughts,' she replied.

Ah, romantic thoughts. We forget, in this age of constant anxiety about the sexualization of the young, that romance used to come first.

At girls' boarding-schools it certainly did, and the notion of romance began with writing poems. We have seen how Miss Alice Baird used to write poems to her head girls each year just before they left St James's, West Malvern. English teachers such as Miss Baird taught their girls to write exhilarated poetry of their preferred kind, using sophisticated metre and lots of caesura, and the girls took to it avidly as an outlet for expressing any kind of rapture. With no boys in sight, the rapture in the early days was often about school improvements. Priscilla Stucley at St James's wrote a poem to the new school swimming-pool:

> *By this mirror of water green and deep,*
> *One might think*
> *To surprise a naiad fallen asleep.*

A St Leonards girl wrote a poem to the new school library, which was installed during her time, in the old house where Mary, Queen of Scots had once lived:

> *Oh you have been a well to me from whence*
> *I drank great peace in deep cool draughts, and*
> *   quenched*
> *The thirst of discontent and pain; and you*
> *Have been a garden full of lovely things,*
> *Among whose flowers I wandered . . .*

This elevated language, enriched daily in the classroom by the study of Shakespeare tragedies and the learning by heart of the poems of Wordsworth and Keats and the whole of Palgrave's *Golden Treasury,* paved the way for the language and behaviour of schoolgirl pashes.

'Oh, yes, pashes,' Sal's sister Georgina Hammick said to me when I reminded her of those long-forgotten schoolgirl adorations. 'I do remember. You wrote poems to their eyebrows.'

It was all rather odd, this schoolgirl falling in love, especially when you consider how unattractive boarding-school teenagers were in the 1940s, '50s and '60s. Their drab uniforms were shaped to make them look as plain and unfeminine as possible, and were quite smelly (the Sunday dresses at St Leonards were known as 'Sunday stinks' because they never went to the cleaners). With their unstraightened teeth (orthodontistry was rare), their plumpness from the starchy diet, their hockey-bruised shins, their chilblains, their spots and their greasy, dandruffy hair washed once a fortnight and roughly towel-dried, these girls were very far from being today's selfie-taking beauties. Their eyebrows were about the only aspect of them that wasn't hideous.

But senior girls were adored, in their entirety, by younger girls. It was called 'having a pash', if you were the lovestruck girl, and 'being pashed on' if you were at the receiving end and fortunate enough to be 'pashable-on'. Pashes were an integral part of boarding-school life, a convention built into the hierarchy: new girls were told by other girls, on arrival at school, that younger girls should have pashes on older ones, and not the other way round. New girls would watch the senior girls filing into the dining-room and try to develop a passion for one of them. Or, as Frances Butler remembers at Wycombe Abbey, the new girl would go up to the older girl and say, 'I've seen you in Chapel. I'd like to have a pash on you, please.' And the senior girl would say, 'OK, that's fine.'

'I have to say, the earth did not move,' Mary James said, recalling the time of her first, dutiful pash on an older girl at St Leonards in the 1950s. 'You had to take her quilt off her bed, and write "so-and-so is divine" on your desk.'

There was no question of ever kissing your pash, or even holding her hand. You just gazed at her from afar, hoping, praying for a friendly glance or a word of kindness. You did sometimes write a poem to her eyebrows and leave it on her pillow. This was preparation, not for adult sexual life, but for the long-drawn-out torment of unrequited love. Unattainability was built into the system. Though the earth did not move for Mary James, for some girls pashes became all-consuming. They were torture: yet another aspect of school life to fill you with anguish and low self-esteem, on top of the agony of worrying about why your best friend in your own year had stopped talking to you, and the constant missing of home, family and pets. Girls would cry themselves to sleep, wallowing in masochistic self-loathing, if their pash had made the tiniest cutting remark to them in passing on the stairs.

But in a strange way, pashes made life at boarding-schools liveable. They gave girls something to think about in a manless environment. They brought the vocabulary of rapture and adoration into the drab world of school breakfast. 'We *lived* on pashes,' said the 1950s Wycombe Abbey Old Girls I spoke to. 'I got a photo of the girl I had a pash on,

Valerie Wheeler,' said Cicely Taylor, 'and I sent it off to be enlarged, and I remember waiting and waiting for it to come back in the post. Valerie played Mr Darcy in the Wendover House Play. Are you *surprised* I had a pash on her?' Pashes were a healthy way of having a figurehead you admired. It was usually the sporty girls with long legs who were the most pashed-on: 'My pash at Cheltenham,' said Mary Villiers, 'was Aline Martell: very good at hockey, in the first team.'

At Queen Margaret's, York pashes were called 'raves', and at St Felix, Southwold and the School of St Mary and St Anne, Abbots Bromley, they were called 'gone-ons'. The person on whom you had the gone-on was 'the gonee'. 'In Chapel, your admirers were looking out for you,' said Tanya Harrod, who was at the receiving end as a senior at St Felix. 'They would offer to empty your waste-paper basket, or they'd give you a note saying, "You looked so wonderful in Chapel today." It was part of the whole language of the way the school worked.'

The girls wrote poems to their adored one, sometimes in sonnet form. It was all part of the aesthetic feel of St Felix: 'bare legs, swimming, art, beauty, the library full of slim volumes by Rupert Brooke,' as Tanya summed it up. At St James's, West Malvern, 'Veronica Waugh left all her strawberries from her vegetable garden in my locker,' said Margeret Redfern. 'And she sewed a handkerchief sachet for me.' These were selfless acts of utter devotion.

Some headmistresses encouraged pashes, understanding that it was a healthy way for girls to let off, if not actual steam, then at least metaphorical steam, and certainly a way to keep them motivated about sewing handkerchief sachets. When Jane Addis developed a deep friendship with Jane Forbes at Tudor Hall in Oxfordshire, the headmistress Nesta Inglis put them in a twin room and didn't mind a bit if they shared a bed. 'We wouldn't have dreamed of touching,' said Jane. 'We just used to lie together and chat. Nesta perhaps wanted us to develop our partnership.' But when Pat Doyne-Ditmas at Cheltenham was caught in the same bath as a friend of hers – again, totally innocently; it was just a matter of saving time and sharing what hot water there was – the housemistress, Mrs Clough, was disgusted and furious. As a severe punishment, both girls were forbidden to go on that term's one and only house expedition. 'Mrs Clough had completely misconstrued what we were doing,' said Pat. 'This innocent event was twisted into something pernicious.'

There was an absolute paranoia among the Misses of the stricter, more buttoned-up schools about any kind of lesbianism breaking out among the girls – even if, as we have seen, it did sometimes break out among the women. Their way of keeping a lid on sexual awakening among their charges was to ban any mention of sex in books, plays or the classroom. In school libraries, pages of books with anything rude on them were glued together: girls would hold them up to the light, trying to glean a single forbidden word. At

Malvern Girls' College, the whole of the Book of Ezekiel was taped together, containing as it does the rudest verse in the Bible. Headmistresses snipped oblong holes in the *Radio Times* if there was an unsuitable word in the title of a programme or its description.

At St Mary's, Ascot, Chaucer's *Wife of Bath's Tale* (on the O-level syllabus) was considered too wicked to be taught by the nuns, as it broke all the rules about the indissolubility of marriage. A lay teacher had to be brought in to teach it. At Penrhos College they taught a bowdlerized version of Chaucer with all the crude bits cut out. Of course, the result of all this censoring was that anything to do with sex became, for the girls, a matter of fascination and helpless giggles.

When, at the Assumption Convent during the war, Catherine Freeman (as Lord Nithsdale) had to speak the lines, 'The first kisses are very sweet to remember, but there is something more in a kiss that has years of love behind it,' and do so while gazing into the eyes of Elizabeth Scotto (Lady Nithsdale), she couldn't get the words out, as both she and Elizabeth simply collapsed into giggles. The drama teacher, Miss Unterberg, a refugee from Nazi Germany and a passionate enthusiast for all the arts, said, 'You *silly* little girls! These are beautiful lines and you spoil them with this foolish laughter.'

In a Greek lesson at Cheltenham in 1949, Miss Biddle made the girls translate out loud a section each of a long passage of Thucydides, going round the class from girl to girl. Pat Doyne-Ditmas saw a terrifying word coming and hoped and prayed she would not be given that section to translate. It was the passage about the plague that killed off a third of the population of Athens in 430 BC, and it described, one by one, the parts of the body the plague infected. The eyes, the nose, the throat, the stomach . . . Pat could see it coming. And sure enough, when the dreaded word came round, it was her turn.

'. . . ran its course through the whole of the body . . . Shall I go on, Miss Biddle?' Pat asked, blushing deep red.

'Yes, please do go on,' Miss Biddle said.

'Even to the . . . er . . . er . . . the genitals . . .'

What could Miss Biddle have said? It would have drawn even more attention to the word, and to her own embarrassment about it, if she had said, 'Please leave out that line.' For both of them, this was an excruciating moment.

In the town of Cheltenham, where girls (as we have seen) were kept strictly apart from boys, not even allowed to walk the same streets, there was bound to be the occasional bit of odd behaviour from the local youths and dirty old men. Occasionally, pornographic photographs would be posted through the front doors of the girls' houses, only to be swiftly disposed of by the housemistress swooping on the doormat. The girls cycled to church at Leckhampton one Sunday and Pat's friend Dumbo, coming out of church, innocently exclaimed, 'Oh, look! Someone's put lots of little balloons in my bicycle basket.'

There was a flasher going about the Cheltenham streets. Miss Popham braced herself and addressed the girls on this subject in Assembly while Dr Herbert Sumsion, the director of music, sat on the platform at the organ, going pink at the ears.

'I'm afraid I have to tell you, girls, that there's a very nasty man about on the streets of the town. I'm afraid he's rather disturbed. I don't want you to take *any notice* of him at all. I want you all to wait until Mr Right comes along.'

To the 800 girls in the hall, it sounded like 'Mr Wright'. Who on earth was Mr Wright?

Poor embarrassed Popeye! Gillian Avery, in *The Best Type of Girl*, tells us that Miss Popham herself (born in 1884) had been under-informed as a child in that department. She had asked her mother, 'Where do babies come from?' and her mother had replied, 'Well, dear, I don't really know. God starts it, and the doctor does the rest.'

Such was the deep embarrassment about anything to do with sex that the staff at girls' boarding-schools in the 1940s and '50s could not bring themselves to tell pupils what really went on between consenting human adults. 'There was a ridiculous lecture once a year for Cheltenham girls aged over 14,' remembers Susie Vereker, 'given by a man called Dr Griffiths. It was a lantern-slide lecture, and it left us none the wiser. It showed a picture of two frogs in a tank of water. One of them jumped on top of the other. Dr Griffiths banged the screen with his stick and said, "There you are! That's it!"' The female staff were so acutely embarrassed by the subject that they brought in a medical doctor to do the explaining; and even he did it badly.

In the year after school certificate, Susie said, there was one more lecture, in the school library, this time about venereal disease and keeping yourself pure for marriage. This enhanced the girls' notion that sex was (a) purely a medical matter, and (b) dangerous. 'Until I got to Oxford I didn't know the facts of life,' Susie said. 'When a man unbuttoned his trousers, I was absolutely appalled.'

If the facts were explained by the Misses themselves, they were couched in terms of the animal kingdom. Even this was almost too much for the women in charge. Susan Beazley remembers the biology mistress at Sherborne School for Girls in the 1940s teaching the class about the alimentary canal of the rabbit. 'As she got lower and lower down the alimentary canal, she started blushing and stammering: she just couldn't cope.' Sherborne was another girls' school with a boys' school in the same town, with similar rules to Cheltenham about separate streets for boys and girls. Such towns seemed to produce the most acute paranoia and embarrassment among the staff.

The only girl I spoke to who learned about the facts of life from the authorities was Marigold Johnson at her farming school – but it was still very much from an animal perspective. 'The older girls used to take the cow to the bull,' Marigold said. 'I never saw it but I heard about it, and I did see a sow giving birth.' Even at the farming school, sex in books was taboo. 'I had a Christmas book-token,' Marigold said, 'and I sent off to Foyle's for a copy of *Jude the Obscure* because I'd heard that Thomas Hardy was a good writer. As soon as it arrived I flicked through it and then hid it as it had a lot of death and sex in it. I knew I'd better keep it quiet.'

Sometimes even animals were too embarrassing to talk about, and another metaphor entirely was adopted. 'We had one rather strange lesson from Sister Maria at St Mary's, Ascot in the 1970s,' remembers Maggie Fergusson. 'She came into our classroom rather nervously one morning and said to us: "I want you to think about what it's like when you go into a bookshop. You buy a really *nice* new book, with a cloth binding and crisp new pages, and you open it and read it with great pleasure. Now, I'd like you to think how preferable that book is to a nasty old dog-eared paper-back that has been read lots of times before."'

It was clear from the way Sister Maria was blushing and looking confused that she was not really talking about buying new and second-hand books. 'That was as close as she got to discussing sex before marriage,' Maggie said. (Luckily, no girl put her hand up and said, 'Actually, I like reading old paperbacks. I like seeing what other people have written in the margins', and so on. Sister Maria would have felt very trapped in her metaphor.)

Girls thus lived in a state of sexual innocence and igno-rance, with their romantic rather than sexual thoughts and their pashes that had no chance of being requited or realized. If their sexuality was burgeoning, this was often subconscious: the 13-year-old Markie Robson-Scott wrote innocently in a letter home to her parents:

Yesterday Beaver and me went to the most super film I've ever seen. It was called Mutiny on the Bounty, and it was in Technicolor, about this chap on this boat with this very harsh captain who flogged the crew all the time. It was heavenly.

Some of the 1950s and early 1960s girls didn't even know what their period was when it started. No one had prepared them: not their parents, not the staff. Embarrassment was too great a barrier to the imparting and receiving of knowledge. 'I thought I had something terribly wrong,' Markie Robson-Scott said. 'Then I had cystitis, which I thought was VD. I felt alone and frightened and didn't even dare tell my mother. I waited till the last day of the holidays before I summoned up the courage to mention it.'

Artemis Cooper noticed a packet of white shiny pads in her drawer at Woldingham and thought, 'How useful! I'll use those for cleaning my shoes.' Sure enough, a week or so later, she took one of these thick pads out of the packet, rubbed it in some black shoe polish and started polishing her clod-hoppers with it. 'A nun came in and was astonished,' Artemis recalls. '"But what are they *for*, if not for polishing shoes?" I asked. The nun replied, "You'll find out soon enough."'

The St Mary's, Ascot girls with time on their hands used to send off to Dr Ruth (the pioneer in sex education), requesting free samples of Tampax. They'd put them into their toothmugs and watch them slowly expand in the water. The nuns did not approve of Tampax, seeing them as dangerously intrusive and penis-shaped.

At St Leonards, if you had your period you were allowed to be off games for three days, as well as being let off washing your hair. You had to go to the housekeeper of your house and ask permission to be off games. It was not the done thing to say, 'I've got my period' or to use the preferred expression 'I've got the curse.' That would have been considered far too blunt. The euphemism to be used was, 'I wish to go in the off-play book, please.' But, as can be the way with euphemisms, even the euphemism became too embarrassing to use. Girls, in agony with period pains, would postpone the dreaded moment of having to ask to 'go in the off-play book' until they were literally doubled up with cramp.

By the 1960s and the Beatles' first LP the truth about the facts of life started to trickle out in dormitories at night. The girls themselves (usually the ones with older brothers who had heard all about it at their schools) filled the gaping vacuum in their friends' knowledge. At Badminton in the 1960s, one girl (the dominant one with a vivid imagination) kept her whole dormitory awake in the first week of term, describing the facts of life in lurid and graphic detail. The quaking new girls, aged 11, homesick enough already, were thrown into the horror of being forced to imagine their parents doing these disgusting things to each other. It was a traumatic awakening.

At schools where discipline was lax and girls had hours and hours of free time, things could get out of hand. At Hatherop Castle, for example, by the 1960s old Mrs Fyfe was losing control. Her problem was, first, that she was going extremely deaf, and the more she fiddled with her enormous hearing-aid the less she seemed to be able to hear; and second, that she trusted the girls too much. If they did anything wrong, she simply said, 'I know you wouldn't have done anything naughty, little lambs.' Hatherop in the 1960s demonstrates what could happen when the lid of repression was lifted and the staff weren't paranoid enough.

The local village boys – known as the 'VBs' for short – simply lined up along the edge of the tennis courts, and behind the squash courts, ready to grab girls when they came off the courts. 'They'd say, "Good evening" in their broad Gloucestershire accents,' said Lizie de la Morinière, 'and you'd have a quick snog.' After lights-out, the VBs hung around at the bottom of the fire-escapes. 'If you sent them down a bra, they'd send up a bottle of cider.'

Rowena Saunders was one of these 1960s girls: she too had been told the facts of life in shockingly vivid detail by another girl on her first three nights at the school. She went down the fire-escape, often, to spend long patches of the night with VBs. 'I used to go out at midnight and stay out till 3 a.m. I was permanently exhausted.'

'At least I got the one I fancied,' said Lizie. 'He was called Dickie. He'd been driving a tractor all day. He grabbed hold of me behind the squash courts. We had a good old French kiss. Then I said, "The bursar's coming!" And he said, '"Night then!"'

Fifty years after leaving the school, Rowena found the telephone number of one of the VBs and rang him up. He was still living locally and still driving a tractor.

To what extent should the headmistresses allow interaction with boys from other schools? This was a dilemma for them. They were worried about the thin end of the wedge – and, seeing what went on at Hatherop, we can understand why. They feared that once you let a few boys in for a Saturday evening social event, the next thing you knew, the girls and boys would be sprawled over the floor of the dining-hall, French-kissing under the portrait of the foundress.

This did indeed happen: Wycombe Abbey girls of the 1970s remember those Saturday-evening discos as being 'like a cattle market'. They dabbed thick layers of blue eye-shadow on their eyelids, and sprayed on Charlie scent, and knew they had to 'get off' with someone in order not to be reviled the next day. The 1970s St Mary's, Wantage girls I spoke to remembered their bitter disappointment on watching a coachload of Etonians getting out of the bus on arrival at Wantage for a rare Saturday-evening disco. They did not look an attractive bunch. 'Don't worry,' someone whispered, 'there's another busload coming.' Nesta Inglis, the headmistress of Tudor Hall, took a liberal tack when she discovered (just after the war) that some of her girls had been meeting a few boys in the garden. 'I'm *so* glad you have made some new friends,' she said to the girls. 'It would be much more comfortable if you could invite the boys to school and we'll have a nice tea-party for them.' There could have been no more effective action taken to put the girls totally off the boys. 'The tea-party,' remembers Jane Goddard, 'was excruciatingly embarrassing and the girls realized these boys were not their cup of tea at all.'

A classroom of St Mary's, Ascot girls in the 1970s dared to broach the subject of interaction with boys with their form-mistress Sister Maria: might she allow them to have an organized event with boys from one of the nearby schools? Possibly to hold a school debate with them? Sister Maria promised to go away and think about it. The next lesson, she came back with her answer. 'You may not realize this now,' she said, 'but girls of your age are *terribly unattractive.*'

This answer showed that Sister Maria had definitely envisaged 'having a school debate with some boys' as the thin end of a wedge that could only lead to much, much worse. Best to avoid the danger altogether.

Mother Bridget told the St Mary's girls that, if they did go to parties and did ever go as far as to sit on a boy's lap, they must never sit directly on his lap, but must always have three pages of newspaper between them. Not one, not two, but three. As Lisa Hiley said, this rule brought a new meaning to the punning 1970s slogan, 'Every woman needs her Daily Mail'.

St Mary's, Ascot sixth-formers did escape from school after lights-out by the 1970s. Julia Wigan used to slip out of a ground-floor window after the nuns had gone to bed. She walked to Ascot station, took the train to Waterloo and spent the whole night (chastely but having great fun) with boys from London day-schools at Charlie's Wine Bar on the King's Road. She would take a dawn train back to Ascot and be back just in time for the nun to put her head into the dormitory and give the daily morning greeting: '*Benedicamus Domino*'. To which the girls, from their beds (Julia's unslept-in), would angelically reply, '*Deo Gratias*'.

15

Future Plans Include . . .

And after all that, what?

Bearing in mind the best-ever example of Old Boys' News understatement – in the Summer Fields school magazine: 'Wavell mi. has done well in Africa' – I flicked through the 'News of Old Girls' pages from the Southover magazine of 1961–2. What were the Southover Old Girls up to after leaving school? Here is a sample:

. . . is doing interior decorating and has been working in a Knightsbridge shop.

. . . has for some time been secretary to Sir Alan Herbert (A. P. Herbert).

. . . is living in Malaya where her husband is in the Army.

... is working in an antique shop in Walton Street.

... is doing a sewing course in Oxford Street.

... is doing a secretarial course in London.

... is working as a shorthand typist.

... is learning French in Paris.

... is learning French in Blois.

... has been in England for a few weeks and went to the Blenheim Ball.

The nearest anyone came to having done well in Africa was '... has done a lot of travelling, including a visit to America and to Kenya.'

Turn the page and you find a list of the latest marriages, all to men with classic British names ... John, Peter, James, Richard, some of them titled, some Major or Lieutenant – and an even longer list of births: 27 births in this magazine, 57 in the next year's one. Quite a crop of babies, when you consider there were only 116 girls in the school. All the Old Girls seemed to be having a lovely time and walking into happy and fertile marriages.

The magazine's Sixth Form Letter, reviewing the year's highlights, mentions that 'Miss Coote came to tell us about the Foreign Office and what the work entailed. We were all very much inspired afterwards, and were determined to try to join the Foreign Office, mainly, perhaps, because the marriage rate is so high!'

By 'join the Foreign Office', the writer did not mean 'pass the Foreign Office Exam and become a diplomat in

Moscow'. She meant 'become a secretary at the Foreign Office'. This was an Old Girl's highest aspiration when it came to jobs, and it was hoped that even that job would be short-lived.

The normal trajectory was: leave Southover at 16, after a final farewell from the headmistress at the door of the drawing-room. (Miss Aspden's final piece of advice, as she saw her leavers off into the big wide world, was, 'You must remember: it is always up to the *woman* to say No.') Then, go to a finishing school for a year, ideally in Switzerland or Paris, but perhaps to Cuffy's in Oxford, or the House of Citizenship in Hertfordshire, to learn French, history of art and how to get out of a car elegantly. Lose weight and go to a hairdresser's. Go with your mother to buy your first ball gown. Be presented at court, otherwise known as 'coming out'. Go to a smart secretarial college in London: Mrs Hoster's or Queen's Secretarial College, where you learned to type in time to the music of the Wedding March. Get a secretarial job at a prestigious place where men had much more senior roles – the Foreign Office, MI5, a famous publishing house, Christie's, Sotheby's or the BBC. Take a great deal of dictation from one of these men. Catch your man; be proposed to; say yes; have a church wedding with a reception at your parents' country house, and your school friends as bridesmaids; discover the facts of life at last; give up the day job; have at least three babies in quick succession; devote your life to being a good wife and mother, and a young grandmother, doing a great deal of voluntary charitable work on the side. Still be married to the same man sixty years later.

'You wanted to get your babies *done* by the time you were 30,' said Linda Cubitt. 'You didn't want to be "old with a fat tummy".' Of the early-1950s Southover girls who were at the lunch in Chelsea that Cecilia Neal kindly gave for me, Linda married at 24, Cecilia at 19, and Cynthia Colman at the ripe old age of 31.

Finishing schools could be the subject for a whole separate monograph, but here are some glimpses of what went on inside them. At Cuffy's in Oxford, the girls were taught French by the erudite 'Cuffy' who had been the French governess to John Maynard Keynes's children. She taught the girls seventeenth- and eighteenth-century French literature and introduced them to the work of avant-garde artists.

'All the princesses of Europe' were at Mademoiselle Anita's in the 16th arrondissement of Paris, according to Brigid Waddams – 'Metternichs, Bourbon-Parmas, Hohenzollerns . . .' There were two classes: *Savoir Vivre* and *Savoir Faire*. *Savoir Vivre* was about manners; *Savoir Faire* was how to deliver a baby. The girls were told, 'You need to learn to do this, because you never know: someone on your estate might need help.' The point, Brigid said, was to pass the time and learn French and some useful accomplishments (including how to deliver the baby of someone on your estate) until it was time to come out or get married.

Riante Rive, on the shores of Lake Geneva, was so strictly

run by its bad-tempered Swiss headmistress that the girls had to 'confess' in a notebook at the end of each day if they had spoken a word not in French. Whenever a boat sailed past on the lake the girls were instructed to turn their backs on it, to prevent any of them so much as looking at a man. They learned how to make a white sauce and iron with a flat-iron warmed on the stove.

'Our parents wanted their daughters to be happy, to make nice friends, to come out,' said Patricia Daunt. 'Then we might have a little job, but the main thing was to get married. A good name, good land, money and title: that was the unspoken aim.' Patricia's trajectory was: spend a year in Paris; go to a secretarial college in London; work as a secretary at the Foreign Office until she was married at 23. She was offered a job at both Christie's and the Foreign Office, and chose the Foreign Office because she wanted to go hunting on the day the Christie's job was supposed to start.

They wore their first jobs lightly, these young women. The great thing about 'jobs' (as Miss Alice Baird called them) rather than jobs without inverted commas, or actual careers, was that you could pick them up, do them for a few months, give them up for the summer and start again in September. 'The jobs only gave you two weeks' paid holiday,' said Cynthia Colman, 'so it was best to give them up, have a holiday, and start a new job.'

Cynthia's trajectory was: finishing school in Lausanne (Pensionnat Les Allières); be a 'double-deb' both in London and America, thanks to the different nationalities of her parents; go to Queen's Secretarial College; work as secretary to Douglas Fairbanks, Jr., 'whose wife started dictating letters to me, to her children at school'. This was the girl who had had her book of Saki short stories confiscated: she was severely under-stretched at Southover.

If they had been born a generation later, these women would have gone to good universities, as their own daughters and granddaughters have. But the posher country boarding-schools of the 1950s, '60s and even '70s, tucked away at the end of gravel drives, were the very last institutions to catch up with the trend of educating girls in a way that made it possible for them to be lawyers, doctors or bankers. The futures planned for these girls, by both the school and their parents, was that they would become the happily married wives of kind, wealthy and successful men from 'good' families: wives who would have time to devote themselves to wifehood and motherhood rather than having to go out and earn money.

Some of my interviewees thought that made for a better, more stable world than today's world of career-ambition, with all the anguish, stress and risky postponement of parenthood it can bring. What hope is there for family life and the glowing heart of the home, they wonder, if women are so busy climbing the career ladder that their households and their children's manners fall into disarray? 'I look at my grandchildren's generation in blind amazement,' said one old Southover girl. 'They have no *intention* of settling down and washing somebody else's socks.'

If you visit girls' boarding-schools these days, the sixth-formers will start handing you their business cards. That kind of thing – and visiting lecturers coming to tell the girls about the exciting job of Investment Banking – would be anathema to my 1950s Old Girls, who were imbued with the idea that their role in life would be one of service to others. Their justification for becoming nurses rather than doctors was, as one of them put it to me, 'I was more interested in the *person* than the disease.' These girls made extremely good, diligent and caring nurses. But what chance had they ever had to think of becoming doctors, with their Bunsen-burnerless education?

We'll see in the next chapter what these women went on to do in later life. Did they settle for the fate determined for them, or did they take their revenge for these low aspirations once their babies and children were done? But first let's look at what was said to the girls when they were still at school, and what was expected of them by their parents.

So many of them would have loved to go to university. Here is what five of them told me, and their stories are typical.

Caroline Dawnay:

Girls at St Mary's, Wantage who went to university were so rare that they had their names put up in gold letters on the panelling in the hall. I was definitely discouraged. The school should have said to my parents, 'Caroline should go to university', but they didn't. When I told my parents how much I wanted to go to university, my father asked his sister to tell me that he'd already spent enough on my education. Many efforts were made to ensure that my brothers went to Cambridge. The real fear was that you were going to be so bright that you would *put men off*.

I left school at 16 and went once a week to a woman who taught me history. I took A-level History aged 16, and English A-level at the British Institute in Florence a year after I'd had my last English lesson. I was allowed to smoke all the way through the exam, and I asked the invigilator if I could have an extra five minutes and he said that was fine.

Then I went to learn to type, and learn to cook, and my mother then wanted to send me to learn to sew, and I had a tantrum about that. It took me a terribly long time – till the age of 27 – to realize that I didn't need to be a secretary or a cook. It wasn't just that the world needed to give *me* permission: I needed to give myself permission. At last it became permissible *to me* to be a literary agent.

Sal Rivière:

It's pretty annoying that no one at Beaufront thought of university for me. When I was married and living in the US, people used to say to me, 'And where did you go to school?', meaning university, and I had to say, 'I didn't.' At finishing school I learned to make a béchamel sauce. It was The Cygnets, in Queensgate. We did have lectures on international history by Guy Hamilton, and he said to me, 'I'm going to write to your father and ask him why you're not at Oxford.' I don't think he got round to writing that letter to my father. I was presented at Queen Charlotte's Ball and then sent to a secretarial college in London, and I got my first job working as a secretary for the War Council in Kenya, taking and typing up minutes for Sir Richard Turnbull, the Minister for African Affairs, and his wife, who were delightful: they continued my education, really, putting me on to good authors. I married at 26.

When I got divorced I worked for a long time in a bookshop in Stow-on-the-Wold. If I'd been to Oxford or Cambridge I could have got myself a proper job: I loved working in the bookshop but it paid peanuts and I was fairly broke. It took me *years* not to be bossed around by somebody.

Diana Copisarow:

My parents went to see Miss Popham [the headmistress of Cheltenham]; they sat in silence for fifteen minutes till she brought out her notes – she didn't have a clue who I was. The school had decided that I wasn't Oxbridge material. My father wanted me to do a secretarial course, 'in case I married a rotter', in which case I would need a secretarial job to fall back on. My mother thought it would be nice to send me to finishing school. I didn't want either. I struck a deal: I would be allowed to go to the University of Perugia for one year to study history of art, Italian and literature. But my mother made sure I lodged with a family – a Fascist professor who had lost his job. I was very, very lonely, and sat in my room with a bed and a basin, and didn't come down except at mealtimes.

Then I 'came out', in London, with my sister. I met my future husband at a coming-out dance. I was the myopic wallflower; he was the man who looked like Byron. We married when I was 19, and we've been happily married ever since. I've been a 'kept woman' for sixty-two years. That was the fashion in those days.

Morar Stirling:

Only one girl went to Oxford during my whole six years at Moira House. I left when I was 17 [in 1951]: I didn't even do Higher Certificate. My father saw no reason why his daughter should go to university. I went to the House of Citizenship, and then to Queen's Secretarial College for a year. Then I got a job at Christie's as a secretary. There I met my husband: he had just come down from Cambridge and was a trainee in the picture department.

Arabella Boxer:

I was very sorry later that I didn't go to university after Hatherop Castle. When I married Mark [Boxer] at 22, all his friends had been at Cambridge and I wished I had.

Part of the problem was that upper-class parents in those days would only accept Oxford and Cambridge – and, at a very long stretch, London – as appropriate universities for their daughters, so girls didn't have much choice: today's options of Durham, Bristol, Edinburgh, Nottingham, Manchester and so on were not seen as suitable for young ladies. Heaven forbid: they might fall in love with a grammar-school boy! Of all my interviewees, only Angela Mackenzie was the exception to this snobbery: her liberal-minded father, the Archdeacon of Leeds, allowed his daughter to go to Leeds University. 'My father said, "I'm going to take you to the university and get you signed up for something. We want you to support us in our old age."' Angela got a place, and the whole school was given a half-holiday in her honour.

About two girls per year got into Oxford from Runton Hall in the early 1950s, but Patricia Bergqvist was not one of them. She won a major county scholarship and was offered a place at Bristol, but her father refused to allow her to go to any university other than Oxford or Cambridge. 'That prejudice was purely, purely social,' she said. 'Public school-boys either went to Oxbridge or into the Army. So I went into the Foreign Office as a secretary and had a fascinating time: I was posted to Beirut and was there during the Suez Crisis. I met my husband there and was married at 24.'

This Oxbridge prejudice persisted right up to the 1970s. 'My father believed there was "the University", meaning "Oxford and Cambridge",' said Virginia Coates. 'He came to see my form teacher nun at St Mary's, Shaftesbury [this was in 1971] and asked her, "Will my daughter be suitable for the University?" She replied, "Probably not". And that was *it*, when I was aged 11. I even had to beg my father to be allowed to stay on for A-levels. His idea was that you educated girls until they were 16 – unless they were suitable for Oxbridge. He put me down for a Leith's cookery course and for Marlborough Secretarial College in Oxford.'

Virginia did manage, aged 23, to get a scholarship for a year's intensive history of art course in London, 'which somewhat assuaged the feeling of having missed out on university, and this led me indirectly into working at Sotheby's'. Georgina Macpherson, a 1970s Heathfield girl, told me, 'My parents told me that if I went to university I could only go to Oxford or Cambridge. Cambridge said to me, "Try again in a year's time", but my parents said "No", so I went to learn to cook.'

It's noticeable in these recollections that it was the fathers more often than the mothers who made the big decisions about their daughters' futures. Deferring to one's husband was still taken for granted in their generation, and flower-arranging wives quietly went along with what their husbands decided was suitable for their daughters. Sons were encouraged to go to university; daughters weren't. Daughters were allowed to get poor results at A-level and drift into being secretaries, cooks and chalet girls until a nice man came along.

Here was what some 1970s ex-Hanford girls said. From lovely, horsey Hanford they had gone on to a variety of unambitious country boarding-schools.

Amanda Graham:

Daddy wanted me to marry someone nice, preferably an Army officer. At Newton Manor I was the only girl to do A-levels. I ended up with one A-level, became a secretary, was married at 23, had children, got divorced. Then I met my second husband, who had been to university, and he gave me confidence. That triggered me to educate myself, and I eventually graduated, aged 40.

Lucinda Mowbray:

Daddy wanted me to get married as soon as he no longer had to pay the school fees. I came top of my year for five years running at Lewiston, but I didn't even do A-levels let alone go to university. I went back to Hanford as a galloping matron; then went to Miss Sprules' Secretarial College in Winchester. I was married at 26, had a child, and divorced three years later. I did eventually do a degree in my forties: I was top of my class again. My son went to Oxford, and I'm sure I could have if I'd been encouraged. To be honest, it has frustrated me so much. I've had PA-type jobs all the way through and you do get fed-up. There was a real sense in those days that 'girls don't matter'.

Some of my interviewees told me they had been suppressed, for years and years, by fathers, schools, husbands, bosses and even sons: a lifetime of submitting to other people's decisions about what they were permitted to try to achieve. It took them decades to come out of their shells.

You can feel it coming: 'except at Cheltenham'. You are right. The choice was: go to a charming, pretty, gentle school and come out knowing reams of poetry by heart but expecting to be a secretary and then a stay-at-home wife and mother; or go to a terrifying, harsh, Gothicky school but at least come out knowing how to do fractions, and with a small possibility of an intellectually challenging career ahead of you.

The cleverest girls at 1950s Cheltenham were groomed for Oxford and Cambridge by its legion of tirelessly strict spinster teachers who expected academic perfection from their pupils. The college library was a haven of scholarly silence in which these future undergraduates learned to think and work by themselves, presided over by a vigilant dragon of a librarian. In this environment, always supported by her father who was ambitious for her education, Pat Doyne-Ditmas got herself to Girton, where she achieved a good Classics degree. But her father then said to her, 'When you leave Cambridge you can have a year at Mrs Hoster's Secretarial College, then you'll be a secretary to a bishop for two years, and then you'll get married.'

So, after all that education, Pat was expected to aim low, as far as careers or 'jobs' went. As it happened, she married before doing either the secretarial course or working for the imagined bishop. But she discovered that the careers open to women, even with Oxbridge degrees, were limited: you needed to 'get your toe in the door' of an august institution such as the V&A or the BBC as a secretary, and then (if you were lucky) you might hop up to a more senior post.

'It was odd,' said Amanda Theunissen, recalling the expectations for pupils at Malvern Girls' College in the 1950s, where the education was excellent and the girls in the top stream 'basically had a boys' education'. 'On Mondays to Fridays, we were taught that we were just as good as boys; but on Sundays, in the school chapel, we were preached at that our aim was to become good wives and mothers.' (The preacher in question was Canon Ronnie Lunt of Malvern Priory.) The headmistress said to Amanda, 'You're intelligent but not academic. I think you'd get a *place* at university, but not a degree.' 'I meekly agreed,' said Amanda, 'and accepted her judgement. I got a job as a temporary secretary at ITN – and that turned out to be the start of a career which led me to being an executive producer.'

Even the cleverest girls from academic schools like Wycombe Abbey didn't get a smooth ride from school to university. They often needed to go to a crammer's for six months to get them up to the required standard.

When the young Elizabeth Butler-Sloss started at Wycombe Abbey in 1946, she announced, 'I would like to be a barrister one day.' The headmistress heard this and said to her, 'In that case, you must do the thanks when we have school events.'

'That was fantastic training,' Elizabeth said, 'learning how to speak in front of a crowd without notes.' She did her Higher Certificate young, aged 16, and tried for Newnham, 'but they didn't want me – and it was Cambridge or nothing for my Cambridge family; no redbrick university would be countenanced'. She went to the University of Lausanne for a year instead, as an external student, to study French, then came home to run the household, as her mother was ill and her father a busy High Court judge. 'My father was wonderful. His view was that I should have the same rights as my brothers. But he did recommend that I should do a secretarial course.'

Elizabeth did this, followed by a two-week placement as a secretary in the City – 'and I was extremely bad at it. My boss said, when I told him I wanted to be a lawyer, "Oh, my dear girl, you can only do better at that than you are at being a secretary."' Then she did the Bar exams in two years at the Inns of Court School of Law. 'There was no doubt,' she said, 'that Wycombe Abbey's teaching got me through.

It taught me to "stick at it". When I became a barrister, in 1955, there were 68 women at the bar and 2,000 men. I took my father out to dinner at Prunier's when I earned my first thousand pounds.'

Many girls' boarding-schools were 'pre-finishing-schools' in those days, Elizabeth said. 'But there was nothing pre-finishing-school about Wycombe Abbey. Not many went to university but you were expected to go and do something in the world.'

16

Boarding-School Women

What struck me, after I had met all these women who went to girls' boarding-schools in the mid-twentieth century, was this: never had I met such a lot of well-educated under-educated women. Especially the older ones. Their book-filled houses, their radios tuned to Radio 4, their kitchen tables piled with old concert programmes and dog-eared copies of the *Times Literary Supplement*, their grand pianos with open music on the stand, the postcards of details of non-obvious Old Master paintings on their chimneypieces, their coffee-table books about the Great Houses and Gardens of Wiltshire, the framed cartoons on the walls of their downstairs loos drawn by a well-known cartoonist as a present for their husband at a seminal moment in his life, the hand-written envelopes on their hall tables, waiting to be taken to the post: these speak of well-read, lively minds, an unflagging zest for life, and taste. They might not know anything about the density of magnesium oxide – the chemistry lessons in the stable block never got that far – but I bet they'd beat today's top-scholarship girl at St Paul's in a quiz on literature and the arts. One thing their education did give them was a lifelong thirst to improve on it.

I have grown to love these women, and, as I mentioned in the introduction, I have learned to spot them. It's partly that you can tell, from their wiry strength, their straight backs, their lack of showy vanity and their slight severity, that they once endured the discomforts, deprivations and petty rules that I have described in these chapters. They learned at a young age, as Josephine Boyle put it, 'to grasp the nettle strongly'. Or, as Mary James put it, 'We learned what we could stand.' This early training in doing things that you loathed, every single day, the moment the bell went, made these women unspoilt, tough and dependable. It has also helped them to get through the worst moments of childbirth and dentistry without making a fuss.

Spending their school-days in stately homes with few creature comforts prepared them well for their adult lives in which many of them have been chatelaines of large, draughty houses with not quite enough home help. They had no difficulties with the belt-tightening days of the 1970s or the 2000s. They were brought up not to expect much in the way of material lavishness. Their sewing-machines are still in use; one old Southover girl said to me that she is still extra-careful when cutting out patterns, ever since the day when a girl in her class accidentally cut the sleeve out of the back of the dress she was making. It is for these women that haberdashers still exist.

I was struck by how many of them still sing in choral societies. The choral backbone of Britain would be a weak thing indeed without them. They enjoy the communal, girls-together life in the second row of the second sopranos, and they always arrive on time for rehearsals. The ones who married diplomats have sung in choirs all over the world, and have even started choirs in far-flung countries that used not to have any. In the alumni magazines of their old schools, where they now appear grey-haired and smiling in group photographs of their year's reunion, they write things like, 'I can still reach top B-flat, or even top C, with the wind behind me!' At the concerts they go to or still sing in, they are still experts at not coughing, because coughing was forbidden in the school chapel.

There is a whole stratum of Kensington and Chelsea Woman, I discovered, a generation older than the ones who install swimming-pools in their basements and have brand-new minimalist kitchens with bar-stools and boiling-water-taps. These are the boarding-school women who have lived in the same house since the late 1950s and have never redecorated the kitchen, so it still has slatted 'Norwegian pine' walls darkened with the patina of fifty marmalade-making Januaries. They even have the original 1950s herb-rack replete with faded 1950s dried herbs.

Though they're sitting on a gold mine, they don't behave as if they are. They keep the heating turned down and put on an extra cardigan when it gets cold. As well as sleeping with the window wide open all year, they still feel guilty if their bath is self-indulgently deep. They cycle or take the bus instead of using the car. Trained in frugality, they don't waste an ounce of food, putting the tiniest leftovers back into the fridge in a bowl, covered with a saucer. At their most extreme, they still abide by their 1950s culinary routine: roast on Sunday, cold roast on Monday, shepherd's pie made by mincing the cold roast on Tuesday, left-over shepherd's pie on Wednesday, soup made from the stock on Thursday, fish (but not disgusting fish) on Friday, salad on Saturday, and back to roast again. They don't like it when their grandchildren are fussy and ask for their carrots to be done in a special way. They say to their grandchildren, 'This is *not* a hotel, and I am *not* a waiter.' Their grandchildren say to them, 'The war's over, you know, Granny.'

Whether they went to a bluestocking boarding-school or to one of the more 'social' ones, most of them have done a great deal of charity work throughout their adult lives, as they were trained to do when gathering round the housemistress on Sunday evenings to knit or sew for the Mission. They were taught to 'give something back'. They said things to me like, 'I've done Riding for the Disabled *for ever.*' Boarding-school women are the self-effacing ones mentioned in votes of thanks at the end of charity balls, when the speaker says ' ... without whose tireless, unflagging work, this evening would not have been possible'. They're the ones who look as if they'd like the ground to swallow them up when they walk up to the dais in their trusty old evening dress to collect the bouquet. 'What – flowers – for *me*?' The most unflagging ones are now MBEs in recognition of their lifetime of dedication.

'In our church,' two old St Leonards girls said to me, 'when the chips are down, the ones you can depend on are the boarding-school girls. When it comes to things like offering to do the tea in the church garden, volunteers write their name down and then fail to turn up! Not the boarding-school girls ... '

It's true that the early marriages to suitable young men did help these women, giving them a leg-up to a contented, stable and well-heeled life: a life that gave them *time* to do charitable work. Wouldn't we all like to be whisked off our feet at 22 by Harold or James or Edward someone and taken to live in an Old Rectory (or manor house or castle) for the rest of our lives? These women were born in the days when that did happen: when you went to work as a secretary in the Foreign Office and did actually find Mr Right there and then. And the romance did come first. And lots of them, from this position of stability and of being loved, having *done* their babies and early-motherhood by the end of their thirties, went on to do Open University degrees in their forties or fifties, or to run businesses. So they did get revenge for the low aspirations prescribed for them. Among my Southover Old Girls, for example, Patricia Daunt has run acclaimed archeological tours to Turkey, and Cecilia Neal has, since her fifties, been running her own successful interior-decorating business. Cynthia Colman did an Open University degree in her fifties, 'but', she said, 'I had to do two foundation courses first, because of my lack of education.'

If, as sometimes happened, and as happened slightly more to the 1960s and '70s girls I interviewed, divorce struck — then what? That was when the bitter wind of inadequate qualifications could really hit you. Aurea Carter (she of the chilblained fingers; West Heath in the 1950s) said that when she got divorced her ex-husband said to her, 'Why don't you have a plate shop, or something?' 'It was meant to be a joke — we're still friends — but I did start a plate shop and it has carried on.' For some, the shock of divorce was the catalyst for a badly needed second dose of education at the local university or higher-education college, leading to a proper job in teaching or psychotherapy.

Those letters waiting to go to the post on the hall tables: to whom are they written? Well, to these women's best friends. And who are their best friends? The girls they were at school with. Great Britain is criss-crossed with a mesh of unbreakable female boarding-school friendships. This was demonstrated to me time and time again when my interviewees said, 'Would you like to come to lunch? I can get eight of us together very easily ...' And sure enough, there they all were a fortnight later, these eight contemporaries who had been in the same dormitory forty, fifty or sixty years ago and who, many decades later, revert to laughing, mistress-mimicking schoolgirls when they get together.

If every long friendship is a weapon for warding off loneliness and depression, we must thank the terms and conditions that brought these friendships to birth. Separation from family, painful though it was, brought the compensation of an early lesson in the value of real friendship and loyalty. The ordeals these women went through together gave them a lifelong bond. Parallel to the Old School Tie network that men make the most of in their careers, boarding-school women have a less lucrative but warmer, gentler network of friendships that boosts their morale and provides balm and sustenance and humour through whatever life might throw at them. They still call each other by their old nicknames.

Some of them were traumatized for life by sadistic matrons saying horrible things to them at times of abandonment. The abject misery of certain desolate moments of their childhood – such as when they saw their parents' car disappear down the drive and knew (aged 8) that they wouldn't see them again for many months, and the matron telling them that very evening that if they carried on howling like that, they'd be put in the kennels with the dogs – had the effect of putting every subsequent sadness in life into perspective. Sometimes these experiences left a trace of ineradicable melancholy. If you were at the receiving end of a quiet campaign of subtle bullying from another girl or group of girls, your trust in other women could be affected for life, and you could suffer from a lifelong fear of not belonging. Women can be awful to other women, as Rosie de Courcy said, with feeling, a propos of DW's icy treatment of her at Lawnside. 'I've come upon it in the publishing world: women as bosses who rule by inconsistency. You know you're out of favour because you get the silent treatment. It's a particularly female form of bullying, and it reminds me of boarding-schools.'

A great deal has been written about English men not being able to relate to other people (even their wives) because they went to harsh boarding-schools where they weren't allowed to cry. Boarding-school women don't seem to suffer from this inability to relate to other people. On the contrary, when together they relate to each other on a deep level, listening intently and giving their frank replies, and this makes for satisfyingly cathartic, putting-the-world-to-rights conversations when you're with them. They discovered that there was nowhere to hide, when you were at boarding-school. Whatever your true character was, it would be found out. So they learned to be honest with each other.

Sitting 'up' at the dining-room table next to the house-mistress or headmistress, they learned to make small talk, asking genteel questions about what the weather was like on

Armistice Day; but together, in dormitories, bathrooms and boot-rooms, they learned to make 'big talk', and this has kept going for six decades. I don't mean that these women let it all hang out in a self-pitying, attention-seeking way as if they were on daytime television. They still retain the strain of emotional austerity that went side-by-side with the physical austerity of their boarding-schools. Though they love each other, they do not see the need to put 'xxx' at the end of their letters: 'Much love from' is quite enough.

I saw the loyal husbands of these older women and it gave me a glimpse of the retired life. When I visited at eleven in the morning, the husband was sent out to do a Useful Errand, and couldn't find his glasses or the necessary ticket. His boarding-school wife (trained in not losing her hymnbook or napkin ring) found it for him, and off he shambled. Sometimes there was no husband as he had died. Husbands so often do die first, I realized. Then, the inner toughness and grit of these women really came into their own. And those lifelong, un-rusted friendships proved their worth. 'I was in an exceptional year of nice and clever girls at Sherborne,' said Susan Beazley. 'Very few of us still have husbands, and we have helped each other through widowhood.'

These women were trained not to see themselves as the centre of the universe, but always to think of others, even when it came to the method for being passed the salt. They learned early that 'it's not all about me'. This lack of self-centredness is, I think, the biggest difference between privileged childhoods fifty or sixty years ago and privileged childhoods today. Yes, these boarding-school girls came from affluent families, but they did not go on skiing holidays every year, and they were not given the idea that things should be arranged mainly for *their* benefit and delight. Their schools taught them that their duty was to be of service to the community: they learned to look outwards and away from themselves rather than to wallow in introspection. Thus they grew into an unselfish, un-self-pitying generation.

The keeping of the lid on their ambitions was, though, shameful: an unimaginative and backward-looking way of keeping women 'in their place' by ensuring that they arrived at adulthood safely under-qualified for anything except a brief secretarial job followed by marriage and keeping house. There was appalling frustration for women in those bad old days. But there can also be frustration for the better-schooled young women of today, who are primed and pressurized from an early age to expect (and feel deserving of) a lifetime of glittering success, and are then profoundly disappointed when they don't achieve it.

The 1960s and '70s old girls I spoke to did not have quite the same level of battle-hardened grit as the 1940s and '50s ones. Life did become a bit more comfortable in those later years, so they did not have to endure such extreme discomforts – though many did (as we have seen) have to endure a pretty useless education. Many of my interviewees from this later batch said to me, 'We've had to rely on our own inner sparkle.'

A typical Heathfield leaver's trajectory in the 1970s would be: do a secretarial course in London; work as a secretary at *Vogue*; do a Montessori course; help out at the Young England nursery school; be a chalet girl in a private chalet; then get married. The age of marriage was creeping up by then, and these girls did need to fall back on their own inner sparkle to find (and put up with actually doing) these first jobs or 'jobs', and then fall back on it again when they needed to find a *raison d'être* after their children went to university. The group of 1970s Heathfield girls I met, brought together at the click of her fingers by Alexandra Etherington and all still extremely close friends, had to negotiate adult life armed with few qualifications. Their inner sparkle and love of fun have got them a long way. Rosie Stancer made the most of her optimism and drive: she became a polar explorer, trekking on her own through the Arctic wastes. 'The seeds were sown at my prep-school, Butterstone,' she told me '– being outside all the time, climbing trees, going out riding in the evenings.'

Those women told me that they were the very last batch of Heathfield girls for whom it was not expected that they would go to university. Virginia Coates (at St Mary's, Shaftesbury in the 1970s) said the same: although she was not given any encouragement to go, 'I did make sure that my younger sisters were able to go to university. I think my year were the last of the girls who didn't automatically go.

At least I did A-levels: quite a few girls didn't even do that!'
The age of the duvet, which comes soon after the end of the
cut-off date of this book, would also prove to be the age of
the female post-boarding-school undergraduate.

The freshness of these recollections of boarding-school life
struck me as forcefully as the wind had once struck my
interviewees on their lacrosse pitches. The very vividness
and rawness of the memories seemed to me proof that the
experiences were traumatic: it's the traumatic memories
from our childhoods that remain the strongest. The very
fact of being torn away from home at a young age and sent
to live in the bracing air of an institution made the memories indelible. I loved hearing how women still think of
and dream about their schools. Erica Burgon told me that
when she and her friends (now in their late eighties) can't
get to sleep, they 'walk through Hinton House', room by
room. (Hinton House was where St Felix, Southwold was
evacuated during the war). Tracing the route from hall to
ballroom to dining-room to staircase calms them and helps
them to sleep.

Angela Mackenzie's memories of the years roaming
the gardens of Castle Howard with the evacuated Queen
Margaret's, York, have furnished her imagination ever since.
'I love being on my own and I put that down to Castle
Howard. I used to go for walks on my own round the lily
pond. You could walk up to the Temple of the Four Winds.
I love trees because of Castle Howard.' All through her adult

life she has used Castle Howard as the imagined backdrop for fiction. 'On the right of the lime walk there was a secret garden: that was the garden I saw when I read *The Secret Garden* to my boys.' The lime walk in *Middlemarch*, the lake in *Sons and Lovers*, the snowy path on which page and monarch went forth together in 'Good King Wenceslas', all these are 'staged' in the Castle Howard grounds as far as Angela is concerned.

As for not having to do games any more, this is still a daily source of relief to the games-haters. So pervasive is the memory of being forced out into the freezing cold every afternoon that women still feel a frisson of dread after lunch on weekdays. 'When the rain's bashing against the windows,' said Caroline Bingham (1950s Roedean girl) 'I still think, "Thank goodness, games just might be cancelled today."' The Sunday-evening melancholy comes back, week after week, so deep is the memory of being wrenched away from home and family after the Day Out, and getting into the cold car, and feeling car-sick as you drew closer and closer to the pair of stone pillars that denoted the border between the outside world and the world you were going back to.

The cruelty, the hopelessness, the cardigans, the chilblains, the filthy food: all these are gone from boarding-schools now. Matrons are kind and motherly and take the girls to the local out-of-town retail village on Saturday afternoons. The catering staff put on Wild-West-themed evenings and serve rodeo burgers. The teachers are happily married: the female ones' bosoms are neither 'out to here' nor 'down to here' but are normal, neither-up-nor-down, happily married bosoms. The classrooms are more in danger of being too hot than too cold. Girls text their parents to report any injustice, certain that their parents will respond at once with a protesting email if they sense any dent in their daughter's happiness. The leavers' results are excellent, most go on to 'uni', the fun is non-stop, the drama is *amazing*, and the girls can choose to do street-dance instead of lacrosse.

This is all marvellous and we live in a better world. But now that fun at schools is so expected, so built in to the daily timetable, is it perhaps less exciting and will it be less vividly remembered?

I can't help thinking that something was lost, when, in the 1980s and '90s, hundreds of small boarding-schools closed down due to lack of pupils and funds. The larger ones needed to smarten up their act in order to have any hope of keeping their numbers up when so many boys' schools were becoming co-educational. Hence the marketing departments, the new sports and drama centres, the television screens boasting of this week's netball victories, the websites that protest (almost too much) that 'research has shown time and time again' that girls work better at single-sex schools.

The smaller schools simply faded away. They closed their doors for the last time after the final prize-giving, and the women who ran them retreated into retirement. The buildings were snapped up by developers and spruced up almost beyond recognition. You can search them: you'll see Southover Manor, Leelands and Ryton Hall divided into well-appointed flats with tidy forecourts lined with low-maintenance shrubs. St Elphin's, Darley Dale is a retirement village, and Sibton Park is 'part of a growing portfolio of fantastic holiday properties across the UK and Europe that are owned by the Holiday Property Bond'. Away, with a few bashes of the builder's hammer, went the junior dining-room, the senior dining-room, the dormitories with their names on the doors, the rows of shelves in the boot-room crammed with Sunday lace-ups.

There was an innocence about these establishments. They were not all about self-advancement or money-making. They were run on a shoestring by women with high moral standards who needed to make ends meet and did so by taking in girls and forming their characters. As much by accident as design, these girls emerged into adulthood with sources of inner strength and resolve that (often literally) can't be measured by exam results. The worst of the hope-lessness has gone, but so have the best of the eccentricity and the most well-meaning of the amateurishness.

In the week when I was writing this last chapter, I happened to drive past Sibton Park in Kent. I decided to turn into the drive, which brought on the inevitable Sunday-evening tightening of the stomach. There it all was, just recognizable but spruced up and eerily devoid of girls in kilts and Fair Isle jumpers doing French-skipping. The back door was ajar and I boldly went in, to be greeted by the faint scent of Mr Muscle spray and not by the smell of fish pie. To the left were the back stairs on which I remember sobbing with homesickness in my first week. I went up them, hoping to find Night Nursery, Day Nursery, Elizabeth Fry and the sick-bay, but all I came to were the closed front doors of two of the holiday flats. Hanging on the wall in the hall, though, were some photographs of the school in its heyday – and there, in the second row of the one from 1975, was the 12-year-old me, pigtailed and squinting at the camera. To the right of me, five or six along, sat 'Marza', the headmistress, her grey hair in a bun.

I heard her voice calling to me across the years. 'Don't go in until the supper bell goes.'

She had said those words to me, firmly and rhythmically, late one summer afternoon, when she saw me practising my under-arm serving in the tennis-courts to the left of the ha-ha wall. I have not forgotten them. When occupied in a task towards the end of a long working day, I remind myself not to go in until the supper bell goes.

I think that quite a few boarding-school women like me still feel a wave of surprised relief each evening, when we remember that we will, in fact, be cooking the supper.

Acknowledgements

Writing this book was made possible by the kindness of my interviewees, who spared me their time and remembered and described their boarding-school days in wonderfully vivid detail. I was also greatly helped by others who suggested people I might speak to and put me in touch with them. Huge thanks to: Jane Addis, Pippa Allen, Nicola Barclay, Anne Barnes, Susan Beazley, Phoebe Berens, Patricia Bergqvist, Caroline Bingham, Arabella Boxer, Josephine Boyle, Charlotte Bradley-Hanford, Fiona Breeze, Fiona Buchanan, Erica Burgon, Morag Bushell, Elizabeth Butler-Sloss, Josie Cameron Ashcroft, Sue Cameron, Sarah Canning, Aurea Carter, Rosemary Chambers, Gillian Charlton Meyrick, Jane Claydon, Virginia Coates, Nicholas Coleridge, Cynthia Colman, Artemis Cooper, Diana Copisarow, Camilla Cottrell, Rosie de Courcy, Amanda Craig, Caroline Cranbrook, Linda Cubitt, Anna Dalrymple, Gillian Darley, Patricia Daunt, Mary Davidson, Caroline Dawnay, Bolla

Denehy, Mary-Ann Denham, Josceline Dimbleby, Sarah Douglas-Pennant, Pat Doyne-Ditmas, Sally-Anne Duke, Sally Echlin, Margaret Ellis, Judy England, Alexandra Etherington, Julia Fawcett, Maggie Fergusson, Charlotte Figg, Serena Fokschaner, Liz Forgan, Sheila Fowler-Watt, Catherine Freeman, Camilla Geffen, Phyllida Gili, Jane Goddard, Amanda Graham, Anne Griffiths, Valerie Grove, Griselda Hailing, Anna Hamer, Rosemary Hamilton, Georgina Hammick, Anne Hancock, Tanya Harrod, Selina Hastings, Louisa Hawker, Anne Heseltine, Lisa Hiley, Clare Hill, Helen Holland, Bridget Howard, Mary James, Sheila Jenkyns, Marigold Johnson, Rachel Kelly, Vanessa Kent, Barbara Kenyon, Judith Keppel, Judith Kerr, Jackie Kingsley, Georgina Lawless, Ann Leslie, Patricia Lombe-Taylor, Jane Longrigg, Laura Lonsdale, Fiona MacCarthy, Jennifer McGrandle, Angela Mackenzie, Georgina Macpherson, Sharon McVeigh, Victoria Mather, Claudia Maxtone Graham, Robert Maxtone Graham, Mary Miers, Lizie de la Morinière, Juliet Mount Charles, Lucinda Mowbray, Cecilia Neal, Sophie Neal, Penny Neary, Georgina Norfolk, Clarissa Palmer, Victoria Peterkin, Henrietta Petit, Georgina Petty, Carole-Anne Phillips, Daphne Rae, Margaret Redfern, Michaela Reid, Gigi Richardson, Sal Rivière, Caroline Robertson, Markie Robson-Scott, Sophia Ruck, Rowena Saunders, Cicely Scott, Barbara Service, Hew Service, Rita Skinner, Gabrielle Speaight, Rosie Stancer, Morar Stirling, Cicely Taylor, Emma Tennant, Amanda Theunissen, Vanessa Thomas, Polly Toynbee, Susie Vereker, Amanda Vesey, Henry

Villiers, Mary Villiers, Miranda Villiers, Brigid Waddams, Francesca Wall, Katharine Whitehorn, Victoria Whitworth, Julia Wigan, Andrew Wilson and Fiona Wright.

I'm very grateful to Gail Pirkis and Hazel Wood at *Slightly Foxed*, who saw the point of this book and welcomed it into existence, chapter by chapter. Thank you also to my husband Michael, always the first to read anything I write.

To buy any of our books and to find out
more about Abacus and Little, Brown, our authors
and titles, as well as events and book clubs,
visit our website

www.littlebrown.co.uk

and follow us on Twitter

@AbacusBooks
@LittleBrownUK

To order any Abacus titles p & p free in the UK,
please contact our mail order supplier on:

+ 44 (0)1832 737525

Customers not based in the UK should contact
the same number for appropriate postage
and packing costs.